81

THE KITCHEN REVOLUTION COOKBOOK

Other books by CEIL DYER:

The Plan-Ahead Cookbook
The Electric Skillet Cookbook
The Hamburger Cookbook
The Wok Cookbook
The Carter Family Cookbook

★

THE KITCHEN REVOLUTION COOKBOOK

★

CEIL DYER

MACMILLAN PUBLISHING CO., INC.

New York

Macmillan Publishing Co., Inc.
866 Third Avenue, New York, N.Y.   10022
Collier Macmillan Canada, Ltd.

Library of Congress Cataloging in Publication Data

Dyer, Ceil.
  The kitchen revolution cookbook.

  Includes index.
  1. Cookery. 2. Menus. I. Title.
TX715.D9774   641.5   80–15544
ISBN 0–02–534530–3

10   9   8   7   6   5   4   3   2   1

Printed in the United States of America

Contents

Introduction

THE COOK HAS ABDICATED, folded her apron, gone on to other, more profitable nine-to-five things. The people have taken over the kitchen, for these days everybody cooks. For some of us it's a sometime thing; for others it's a day-in, day-out part-time job. The "hate to cook" school of cooking is passing: it's no longer fashionable to be the fluttery little woman who can't boil an egg, and no one is amused by that bachelor who simply can't cope with a stove. The high cost of food has made good cooks of us all, but not in the same old set ways. A revolution in the kitchen has indeed taken place. The way we live now has changed the very way we cook. New equipment and new ideas about what really is good food have pushed our old concepts about cooking into the discard. Finally, for the first time, there is a new, truly American cuisine. Weight-conscious, health-conscious Americans no longer follow outdated European ways. We love good food and we cook it, some of the best in the world, but though in part adapted from other countries, the food we cook is now uniquely our own.

This book is about the new American cuisine. It presents recipes which are made possible by the new equipment in our kitchens and which use the new, to most of us, ingredients that have suddenly begun to appear on every supermarket's shelves. It provides realistic menus based on how we really eat in these fast-paced, ever-changing days.

It's easy cookery and it's fast (who has time for anything else?), it's nutritious, and it's prepared with one eye on the calorie chart. But most of all, it's simply delicious food.

There are no menus here for the old blue-plate special of meat,

ix

potatoes, two vegetables, and dessert; there are no recipes for a main dish that must have a supporting cast of time-consuming side dishes; there are no laborious desserts that seem designed more to impress than to please the taste. Instead, with the exception of breads and desserts, every recipe is a main dish. What is to be cooked or prepared for tonight's dinner depends on the mood of the cook and the appetite of the diners. Tonight a soup or a salad may be the main course. If it is to be slightly heavier fare, a stir-fry of vegetables and meat or a complete dinner from a skillet may take the place of honor.

And while we have learned to cook what we want, we have learned to eat when and where we want. Supper on a warm summer evening could be a big salad served on the porch; a dinner party could be a stir-fry served in the kitchen. Or dinner could be an "eat when you please" kitchen meal of a great soup kept hot in an electric slow cooker. This is not to say that the more stylized dinner of two or three courses served on a well-set table in the dining room has vanished from our lives. Far from it—there are times when nothing else will suffice. But it's no longer an everyday routine, simply because it no longer fits the everyday routine of our lives.

So the kitchen revolution has produced what all good revolutions should produce: freedom. Freedom to cook, eat, and enjoy the kind of food that suits our needs, our tastes, our time, and our pocketbooks; whether it be a truly great sandwich or a lavish English mixed grill. Both fit our pattern, for in truth there is no pattern—simply good food, easily prepared, and served how, where, and when we want it.

Every recipe in this book has been created to liberate the cook, but only from time-consuming, unnecessary chores. Devotion to great taste and to memorable eating has not been sacrificed to the gods of speed and price.

The New Power
in the Kitchen

It seems that almost every month brings us another power tool for the kitchen: processors, blenders, mixers, grinders, pasta makers, convection ovens, microwave ovens, broilers, toasters, ice-cream freezers, espresso machines, ice makers, etc., etc., etc. Few kitchens could hold them all, few cooks would want every one. But what to choose? Which are the most useful? In short, which ones are worth their not inconsiderable price?

The answer, of course, is none of them or all of them; it depends entirely on how you cook and what you cook. For example, if you live in a large city where really good bread is readily available from a baker and you do not enjoy making your own bread, a super mixer with a dough-hook attachment will only gather dust in your kitchen. How much you use and enjoy any of the new equipment that has followed in the wake of the kitchen revolution determines its worth to you, and only you can make the decision.

While testing the recipes for this book, I have used just about every new piece of equipment American expertise has devised. The truth is, every one of them "delivers the goods," i.e., the machine performs as promised, and in most cases, even better than promised. But no machine can cook for you; it can only work for you. Delicate shrimp quenelles are still a lot of work even for the skilled cook. A processor will make the task easier, but quenelles will always be more complicated than a hamburger. In short, the machine will only do what you ask, and the results will be only as good as your recipe and your skill at the stove.

With this sobering thought in mind I give you my personal evaluation of some of the newer appliances, in the hope that it will be of some help to you in making the right decision before you buy.

FOOD PROCESSOR: This year's queen of the kitchen counter: indispensable for making pâtés, mousses, quenelles; chopping meats (the best hamburger I ever ate); grating such hard-to-grate ingredients as Parmesan cheese or fresh coconut; chopping quantities of onion or green pepper; cutting wafer-thin slices of potatoes, carrots, zucchini, or any firm vegetable; incorporating lemon rind or vanilla bean into sugar for cake making; making cream puffs; and simply great for slicing cucumbers for pickles. For small jobs, however, it's more trouble than it's worth, i.e., it's easier to mince a little parsley with a sharp knife on a cutting board than to process it and then wash and dry the processor. As for slicing soft fruit or vegetables like strawberries or tomatoes, a small sharp knife is a better choice. A processor can replace an electric blender on your kitchen counter, since it blends and purees to perfection. But, and I guess there is always a but, it has limitations. It will not whip cream or egg whites: for these a rotary beater or French wire whisk is indispensable. While the processors do knead bread dough, their containers are not large enough to make more than one loaf, with the notable exception of Cuisinart's new D.L.C.-7 model. Although the makers claim it's great for mixing cake batters, I found that unless you are extremely careful the double-fast speed will over-mix, resulting in a heavy-textured cake or, what is worse, a complete failure: misshapen and uneven, a total disaster. To sum up, if bread and cake making are only a "sometime thing" in your kitchen, you may find that a processor can take over most of your most tedious kitchen chores. One note of caution: don't try to get a "bargain" when you shop for a processor. The machine is only as good as its motor, and light, cheap power simply won't do the job. I have used Cuisinart, General Electric, and Waring processors with success; all three have performed admirably.

THE DO-EVERYTHING MACHINE: The Kitchen Aid K5A is the best known. Following on its heels are the Bosch Magic Mixer and the Braun Kitchen Machine; a less serious competitor is the

Sunbeam Mixmaster. The K5A has been my kitchen companion while writing this book, and it is indeed a strong contender for first place on the "must" list of dedicated cooks. This machine will do literally just about anything the cook could ask except cook the food: kneads sufficient dough for up to six loaves of bread, easily mixes heavy batters such as those for pound cake and fruit cake, whips cream and egg whites to unprecedented heights. It grinds meat; grates cheese and nuts; makes sausage, pâtés, and meat spreads; shreds and slices meat and vegetables. Available attachments include juice extractor, colander, and a sieve for use in canning and preserving. There's even a grain mill attachment that grinds wheat, corn, rye, oats, buckwheat, and barley. Now if that isn't enough, there's even an attachment for polishing your silver.

If the K5A sounds like "a bit much" (it is a big, heavy-duty machine and has to be), both the Bosch Magic Mixer and the Braun Kitchen Machine will perform many but not all of the same functions, while taking up less space in your kitchen. However, if bread and cake making are the primary uses to which you will put this type of machine, then the Sunbeam Mixmaster with a dough hook might be an excellent choice, at a much less formidable price. Ultimately, the decision depends on just how much you want the machine to do. As with any appliance, its value lies in the extent to which it is used.

THE ELECTRIC SLOW COOKER: A "can't do without" appliance for any cook who also holds down a nine-to-five job. Whole meals can be assembled in the cooking pot before leaving for work, turned on, and left until serving time that evening. A real fuel saver, it's great too for beans, soups and stocks, and anything that benefits from long, slow cooking.

GRILLS AND ROTISSERIE BROILERS: The portable type of range, from small units that will grill a cheese sandwich or a hamburger to the deluxe large size (Farberware makes an excellent one) that can handle a mixed-grill dinner or roast a chicken on its rotisserie attachment. They can be part of your new Jenn Air stove—that ultimate cooking system—or they can be outdoor equipment for use with charcoal or bottled gas. If you, like most Americans, like what we call barbecued food, cooked over intense heat, you will find a grill sufficiently large to cook a total meal a real joy to own. It fits nicely into our current way of cooking since it makes quick, easy, fun-to-eat meals; if you prefer a casual entertaining style, buy the best you can afford: you won't regret a penny of its purchase price.

PORTABLE CONVECTION OVENS: Newest of the counter-top ovens, the convection cooks by means of hot air circulating rapidly around the food.

Faster than a conventional oven, the convection will usually cut cooking time by one-third.

Portable convection ovens have recently been introduced by Cuisinart, Farberware, Maxim, and Moulinair. All operate on the same principle, all are equally easy to clean, and all three cook with equal efficiency. The Farberware oven, however, has a larger capacity than its competitors without taking a corresponding larger amount of space on your counter. I also found the Farberware design easier to handle. Convection ovens are also available as part of some of the newer stoves, notably Jenn Air, but if your aim is to add to your present equipment, the portable variety will do the job handsomely. It is particularly useful for defrosting and heating frozen foods, cooking bacon or breakfast sausage to perfection, and heating rolls or bread.

The convection particularly shines in cooking a roast: the meat browns to a turn on the outside and is pink and juicy within. Just remember that it cooks in about one-third less time, so check your recipe and adjust accordingly. Incidentally, the usual grease-spattered oven that is the inevitable result of roasting in a conventional oven is happily absent with a convection.

The convection oven will also roast frozen meat from start to finish in about the same time needed for defrosted meat in a regular oven. This is a real convenience for the after-hours cook. However, a convection oven cannot replace your regular oven entirely. Convection cooking retains moisture within the food, which is fine for meats or foods that might dry out if cooked in a conventional manner, but it is a problem when baking rich cakes or breads, cookies, or fruit-filled muffins. Buy a convection oven if you have the space for it or need an extra oven. It's great too for party meals, and particularly useful for defrosting and heating frozen foods (your own or commercially prepared). For my money it's worth its price for roasting meats alone.

MICROWAVE OVENS: Even the manufacturers of the microwave tell me, "It takes getting used to." In other words, learning to cook with a microwave takes time. But it took time to learn many other methods of cooking, so why not? If you want to save time, if your primary goal is to cook quickly, a microwave may be for you. If, however, your first objective is to prepare the best-tasting, most appetizing food possible, then think before you buy. If you have a freezer full of frozen convenience foods or if you work and need to buy time, a microwave can be just what you need. But don't expect to use it for grilling or roasting satisfactorily, or for making a delicate sauce, a rich-tasting stew, or any other combination of foods that needs slow, moist heat to bring out and combine flavors. A microwave can be a satisfactory buy if you accept its timesaving factors with its equal limitations.

ICE-CREAM MAKERS: Hardly an essential appliance, but since ice cream is apparently everybody's favorite dessert you just may decide to own one. Basically there are three types on the market. The first is virtually the same as the old-fashioned hand-cranked churn that used to grace the back porch: the only difference is that there is now a motor on top and one has only to plug it in instead of laboriously turning the crank by hand. The best known of this type is made by White Mountain, a company that has been making ice-cream freezers (nonelectric, of course) for over 100 years. The second is a small unit that must be placed in the freezer and then plugged into a nearby socket. The wire goes through the freezer door opening—in my opinion a scary operation, since it has not been approved for safety by the Underwriters' Laboratories. The third, a new contrivance by Waring, is a small, efficient machine appropriately named The Ice Cream Parlor. This makes two quarts of ice cream and uses only two trays of ice cubes plus regular table salt. The Ice Cream Parlor is compact, easily washed and stored, and has performed admirably in testing the ice creams and sherbets in this book.

COFFEE MAKERS: The Automatic Drip coffee pot that employs a filter paper has swept the country; best known is probably "Mr. Coffee," which has a bevy of competitors. All of these make excellent coffee, since the use of a filter and the principle of a single-pass-through method assure a strong, clear brew. However, to my mind the Chemex nonautomatic drip coffee maker (which also employs a filter paper) makes a superior brew, for two reasons. First, the Chemex is extraordinarily easy to keep clean, an absolute necessity if the bitter taste of rancid coffee oils is to be avoided; second, the design of the Chemex pot is such that the coffee can be kept hot only by placing the pot in a second pot of very hot water. Troublesome, but it is the only way to keep the coffee hot without burning it. The far lower price of the Chemex is only an incidental pleasantry.

For true coffee fans there is a new espresso machine on the market that has become the joy of my life, the Salton Espresso Machine. Until the advent of the Salton I had confined my passion for espresso to Italian restaurants of the better sort. The various espresso pots previously on the market were either ersatz, i.e., actually drip pots that employed dark roast coffee for the effect of espresso, or extremely complicated and/or very expensive true espresso machines that, very frankly, belonged in a restaurant, not on a kitchen counter. The Salton is both simple and safe to operate and exceptionally easy to keep clean, a must with all coffeepots to avoid rancid oil buildup. It makes up to six cups of fragrant real espresso and if desired will make frothy cappuccino as well.

CATCHALL: There are of course literally dozens of other appliances to speed the cook's efforts, smooth the cook's path, or simply take your money. The pasta machine is useless unless you are impassioned about homemade pasta; the toaster, no matter how good-looking, will only gather dust if you don't like toast. The electric can opener will stay unused if you find (as I have) that it's too difficult to clean, and so on down an almost endless list of household products. Not that each cannot be useful to some cooks, but all are seldom desirable. I personally cannot do without my electric coffee grinder, but I find an electric skillet not as efficient as my nonelectric wok. Freedom of choice is the cook's prerogative, and it is indeed a marvel to have so much to choose from. Just be sure you *decide* what to buy; don't let the manufacturer decide to *sell* it to you.

THE KITCHEN REVOLUTION COOKBOOK

Soups

THE FOOD PROCESSOR, the blender, and the electric slow cooker have put homemade soups back in style. And make no mistake, homemade flavor can never come out of a can or from a packet of mix. Soups can be made processor-fast in minutes, or they can simmer for hours in time-honored soup-kettle fashion. But there is no need for the cook to simmer along with the soup; the slow cooker takes over unattended for as long as is necessary. The days of stirring and watching are over. As for the super-speed processor soups, nothing could be better tasting, faster, or easier; proof enough that truly good food need no longer make a slave of the cook.

Nor is soup still just the preamble or the overture. Good soup *is* the meal, and a great one. Included here is a suggested menu for each of our soups, to make the most of a good thing. For there is no time when the right soup isn't welcome, no time when soup doesn't do some good. If you are "starving," a hearty soup satisfies as nothing else can; if your appetite flags on a summer day, icy cold soup is as welcome as a shade tree; and nothing chases the chills of winter faster than a steaming bowl of well-seasoned soup.

We begin with a collection of five-minute wonders (ten minutes, if you're slow), as good as any soup you ever tasted, made with the help of your processor or blender in less time than it takes to read the recipe. Next, a heartwarming group of slow-cooker specialties with all the deep-down homemade taste of slowly cooked soup but made without old-fashioned home-made work.

1

DOUBLE-QUICK SOUPS

The miracle of these soups is the way in which simple and inexpensive ingredients are transformed into beautiful soups with deep, rich, satisfying flavor in a matter of minutes; a food processor (or blender) does the trick. You can start, if you have them on hand, with homemade stock and fresh vegetables just picked from your garden, which would of course be perfection. But I don't mind relying, when necessary, on top-quality canned and frozen substitutes. Using canned chicken broth and frozen peas, for example, I can make a superb Cream of Curried Pea soup in less than six minutes. It would take hours if I started from scratch.

Cold Cream of Chicken Soup Senegalese

> 3 cups chicken stock or broth, well chilled
> 1 small tart apple, peeled, seeded, and chopped
> 1 to 3 tsp. Madras curry powder
> 1 cup heavy cream, well chilled
> Salt to taste
> White pepper to taste
> Minced chives or paprika

Place 1 cup stock or broth in electric blender or food processor. Add apple; blend or process to a smooth puree. Add curry powder and cream; blend briefly. Season to taste with salt and pepper. Add to remaining chicken stock. Pour into chilled bowls. Sprinkle with chives or paprika. Serve at once.

NOTE: Soup may be made ahead and refrigerated until time to serve. Just before serving, reblend briefly but well, 2 cups at a time, in blender or processor.

WARM WEATHER
LUNCHEON-PARTY SUGGESTION

Cold Cream of Chicken Soup Senegalese
Italian Bread Sticks
Brie Cheese and Ripe Pears
Raspberries or Blueberries with Cream
French Gaufrettes
Coffee

Corn Chowder

    2 Tbs. chopped green onion
    2 Tbs. butter
    2 cups fresh corn kernels or 1 (10-oz.) package frozen
      corn kernels
    1 thick slice Italian-style bread, cut into cubes
    1 cup chicken broth, canned or homemade
    1 cup milk
    2 Tbs. dry sherry
    Salt
    Pepper to taste
    Dash Tabasco sauce

In a soup pot sauté green onion in butter until soft. Add half the corn and cook, stirring, until heated. Scrape contents of pot into work bowl of food processor (or electric blender); add bread cubes and broth or stock, process (or blend at high speed) until almost smooth. Pour mixture back into pot, add milk, remaining corn, and sherry. Place over medium heat, stir until heated. Season with salt, pepper and Tabasco. Serve very hot. *(See Menu Suggestion on p. 4.)*

    • *Makes 4 servings.*

NOTE: This is a delicate, hearty soup, if such a contradiction is possible. If you wish and can afford it, add a pint of small oysters and their liquid to the hot soup, stir until oysters are heated, lace with a little more sherry. Call it corn and oyster chowder, of course. It's superb.

MENU
SUGGESTION

Corn Chowder
Thin-sliced French-style Bread Spread
with Soft Butter
Cold Baked Ham Slices
Peach Halves with Chutney (broiled
until bubbly hot)
Iced Tea, Fresh Mint
Slices of Poppy-Seed Cake (see p. 147)
Coffee

Cream of Curried Pea Soup

> 1 (10-oz.) package frozen peas or 2 cups cooked fresh peas
> 1 small ripe pear, peeled, cored, and coarsely chopped
> 2 sprigs parsley, stems removed
> 2 green onions, coarsely chopped
> 1 to 2 tsp. Madras curry powder
> 1 cup chicken stock, canned or homemade
> 1½ cups milk
> ¼ cup heavy cream
> Salt
> Pepper
> Minced chives (*optional*)

Put frozen peas in a colander under hot running tap water until they feel defrosted.

Combine peas, pear, parsley, green onion, curry powder, and stock in work bowl of food processor or in electric blender. Process (or blend on high speed) until smooth. Transfer mixture to top of a double boiler; add milk and cream. Place directly over medium heat and bring to boiling point, stirring almost constantly. Season to taste with salt and pepper. Put the pot over simmering water and let soup steam for 2 to 3 minutes to develop flavors. Sprinkle with minced chives if desired. Serve very hot.

• *Makes 4 to 6 servings.*

MENU
SUGGESTION

Cream of Curried Pea Soup
Grilled Cheese and Chutney Sandwiches
Peeled, Sliced Navel Oranges Sprinkled with Kirsch
Coffee

Black Bean Soup

1 small white or purple onion, peeled, minced
2 stalks celery, trimmed, minced
2 Tbs. butter
2 cups cooked (dried) black (turtle) beans *(see p. 13)*
2 cups chicken stock or broth, canned or homemade
½ to 1 cup shredded lean cooked ham
Salt
Freshly ground black pepper
1 Tbs. red wine vinegar
Paper-thin lemon slices

In a soup pot sauté onion and celery in butter until soft. Scrape mixture into work bowl of food processor; add the beans and ½ cup of the stock, process until smooth (or do this in an electric blender). Transfer mixture to soup pot; add remaining stock and ham. Place over medium heat and stir until boiling point has been reached. Season to taste with salt and pepper. Reduce heat and let soup steam a few minutes to develop flavors. Just before serving stir in vinegar. Float a thin slice of lemon on top of each serving.

• *Makes 6 servings.*

MENU
SUGGESTION

Black Bean Soup
Onion Sandwiches
Chocolate Strawberries (see p. 161)
Coffee

Cream of Spinach Soup with Cheese

¼ lb. provolone cheese
1 (10-oz.) package frozen chopped spinach, cut into chunks
¼ cup boiling water
1 thick slice Italian-style bread, cut into cubes
1 cup chicken broth or stock, canned or homemade
1½ cups milk
Salt
Garlic salt
Pepper

Coarsely grate cheese in food processor. Remove and set aside.
(Or grate cheese on hand grater.) Put frozen chunks of spinach
in food processor, pour in boiling water. Let stand until almost
thawed. Add bread cubes and stock or broth; process until
smooth (or do this step in electric blender at high speed). Pour
mixture into a saucepan, add milk. Heat to almost boiling; add
salt, garlic salt, and pepper to taste. Cook, stirring, over low
heat 2 to 3 minutes. Pour into deep bowls. Spoon grated
provolone cheese generously over each serving and serve at once.
• *Makes 4 to 6 servings.*

MENU
SUGGESTION

Cream of Spinach Soup with Cheese
Italian Breadsticks
Marinated Tomato Slices with Chopped Parsley
Peanut Butter Cake (see p. 143)
Coffee

Watercress Soup

1 bunch watercress; use leaves and tender stems only
2 or 3 green onions
1 stalk celery

1 tart apple, peeled, cored, coarsely chopped
3 cups chicken stock or broth, canned or homemade
½ pt. heavy cream
Salt to taste
Watercress leaves

Put watercress, green onion, celery, apple, and 1 cup chicken stock or broth in work bowl of food processor; process until smooth (or use electric blender). Pour mixture into a saucepan, add remaining stock or broth, bring to a boil, lower heat, let simmer 3 to 5 minutes. Stir in cream, season with salt. Stir until steaming hot.* Garnish individual servings with watercress leaves.

• *Makes about 8 servings.*

*May also be chilled and served very cold.

MENU
SUGGESTION

Hot Watercress Soup
Bread and Butter Sandwiches
(use a good firm, hopefully homemade bread)
Ripe Brie or Camembert with Crackers
Dry White Wine
Cherry Torte (see p. 148)
Coffee

Borsch

1 small purple onion, peeled, chopped
1 stalk celery, chopped
2 Tbs. butter
1 (1-lb.) can sliced beets
3 cups chicken broth or stock, canned or homemade
Juice from 1 large lemon (about 3 Tbs.)
Salt
Pepper
Sour cream
Red caviar *(optional)*

In soup pot, sauté onion and celery in butter until soft. Scrape contents of pot into work bowl of food processor; add beets and beet liquid; process until smooth. Pour into soup pot, add stock, heat to boiling. Lower heat, let simmer a few minutes to blend flavors. Add lemon juice, season with salt and pepper. Serve hot with a dollop of sour cream on top of each serving. If you feel expansive, sprinkle sour cream with a bit of red caviar.

• *Makes 4 to 6 servings.*

NOTE: This soup is equally good served icy cold. Chill in refrigerator, then reblend in processor or electric blender just before serving.

MENU
SUGGESTION

Hot Borsch with Sour Cream
Sandwiches of Black Bread, Butter, and Cucumbers
Pears and Stilton (see p. 161)
Dry White Wine

SLOWER-COOKING SOUPS

French Onion Soup

The ultimate soup, deep amber in color, fragrant with the essence of onion, and made the time-honored way: an abundance of onions simmered for hours.

9 cups chicken stock or broth, canned or homemade
3 medium-size, mild purple onions, peeled and sliced
Salt, if desired
Thick slices crusty French-style bread
Freshly grated Gruyère or Parmesan cheese

Put stock and onions in slow-cooking pot. Cook on high setting for 1 hour. Cook on low setting 12 to 24 hours (cook on high setting for final hour). Season if needed with salt. Ladle over thick slices of crusty bread in deep soup bowls. Sprinkle generously with grated Gruyère or Parmesan cheese.

• *Makes about 8 cups soup.*

MENU
SUGGESTION

Onion Soup
California Cabernet-Sauvignon
Apples   Ripe Brie   Thick Slices French Bread (lightly toasted)

Potage Parmentier

(Leek and potato soup)

> About 3 baking potatoes, peeled and cut into 1-inch chunks
>   (approximately 3 cups)
> Leeks, white part only, thinly sliced (approximately 1 cup)*
> 6 to 8 cups water
> Salt
> White pepper
> Curry powder (*optional*)
> Dash Tabasco sauce (*optional*)
> Milk or heavy cream (*optional*)

Put potatoes, leeks, and water in slow-cooking pot. Cook on high until potatoes are very tender, about 2 hours. Remove potatoes with a slotted spoon and place, about ⅓ at a time, in work bowl of food processor; process very briefly, only until pureed. What you want to achieve here is a slightly grainy and thick puree. Return potatoes to soup; place on low setting. Add about 1 tsp. salt. Taste, add additional salt and pepper if desired. Add a small amount of curry powder, 1 tsp. or a little less, and a dash of Tabasco. Leave on low setting until ready to serve. Just before serving add a little milk or use heavy cream if you like. *(See Menu Suggestion on p. 10.)*

• *Makes 6 to 8 servings.*

*If leeks are not available or prohibitive in price use large, bulbous green onions (which makes this another soup entirely but one that is, to me, just as good).

Here is a classic example of "less is more." Most American cookbooks have "refined" this basically honest peasant soup by preparing it with chicken or beef stock, which changes it completely; the earthy flavor of the potato is lost and along with it much of the soup's character.

NOTE: This recipe is the basis of vichyssoise, that most elegant of cold soups. Prepare the soup as above, refrigerate until chilled. Stir in about 2 Tbs. heavy cream for each cup of soup. Blend and serve in chilled bowls. Sprinkle just before serving with finely minced chives (if chives are not available the finely chopped tops of green onions will substitute nicely).

FURTHER NOTE: Other vegetables may be added to the basic soup. For a beautiful pale green soup, add 1 cup well-washed spinach leaves the last 5 minutes of cooking. Puree as directed; serve hot or well chilled. Or use cooked green peas or chopped lettuce.

MENU
SUGGESTION

Potage Parmentier
Toasted French Bread
Apples with Sharp Cheddar Cheese
Dry White Wine

Italian Vegetable–Bean Soup

This is the most gorgeous soup, a true inspiration from southern Italy.

    1 lb. dry white navy beans
    2 to 4 qts. water
    1 large baking potato, peeled, cut into cubes
    2 medium carrots, peeled, cut into small dice
    2 large tomatoes, peeled, chopped
    1 mild purple onion, peeled, finely chopped

2 medium zucchini, trimmed, coarsely chopped
½ lb. fresh string beans, trimmed, cut into 1-inch lengths
Salt
Pepper
¼ tsp. mixed Italian herbs

Parmesan parsley
¼ lb. Parmesan cheese
Parsley, finely minced, sufficient to make about ½ cup,
   packed down

Place beans in a colander and rinse under cold water until water runs clear; place in slow-cooking pot. Add 3 qts. water, soak overnight. Next morning, cover, cook on low setting 4 to 5 hours. Add all vegetables, about 1 tsp. salt and Italian herbs, cook on high setting until vegetables are tender. Taste, season with pepper and, if necessary, additional salt. Serve very hot, each serving sprinkled generously with Parmesan parsley.

To prepare Parmesan parsley
Grate cheese. Combine with parsley.

SUMMER-DAY
LUNCHEON SUGGESTION

Raw Mushroom Slices in Vinaigrette Sauce
Ripe Olives
Italian Vegetable–Bean Soup
Italian Bread
Lightly Chilled Beaujolais
Strawberry Clafouti (see p. 157)
Coffee

Vegetable Soup

This is a true vegetable soup, superior in my opinion to so-called vegetable soups that are dominated by the flavor of a meat base.

2 or 3 ripe tomatoes, peeled, quartered
1 or 2 small zucchini trimmed, cut in half, halves cut lengthwise into thick pieces
1 clove garlic, peeled, minced
1 carrot, scraped, sliced
1 small turnip, peeled, chopped
1 large onion, peeled, chopped
2 stalks celery, chopped
Water
3 or 4 leaves fresh rosemary or 1 tsp. dried rosemary (crushed), or use fresh or dried basil
1 tsp. salt, more if desired
¼ tsp. pepper, more if desired
½ to 1 cup chopped fresh spinach
½ to 1 cup cooked lima beans
Parmesan cheese

Put all the raw vegetables except spinach and lima beans in a slow-cooking pot. Add water to cover by about 2 inches. Season with herbs, salt, and pepper. Simmer on low setting for 4 to 6 hours. Add the spinach and lima beans. Cook a few minutes longer.

• SERVINGS: *It will fill 4 to 6 nice-size soup bowls with a bit left over.*

NOTES: This, of course, is a loose recipe; you can add or substitute other vegetables. For a thicker soup, add a peeled and diced potato or about ¼ cup raw rice. Use shredded romaine lettuce instead of the spinach, and instead of the lima beans or along with them add about ½ cup small noodles or other pasta; serve the soup Italian style with grated Parmesan or Romano cheese and crusty Italian bread.

FESTIVE SUNDAY-NIGHT
SUPPER SUGGESTION

Melon Slices with Prosciutto
Vegetable Soup
Hot Corn Sticks
Flaming Cherry Tart (see p. 158)
Coffee

Black Bean Soup for a Crowd

This is a wonderful main dish for a buffet supper party.
Accompaniments could include a "make your own" sand-
wich tray of assorted cold meats and a variety of breads,
followed by a bowl of fresh fruit and a platter of cookies.
Coffee, of course, to wind up a great meal.

1 lb. dried black beans
3 qts. cold water
1 large onion, peeled, chopped
1 clove garlic, peeled, minced
2 stalks celery, chopped
2 carrots, scraped, chopped
A ham bone
1 cup chopped leftover baked or boiled ham
Salt
Pepper
½ cup dry sherry

In slow-cooking pot soak beans overnight in water to cover.
Drain; add the 3 qts. water and remaining ingredients, except
sherry. Cover and cook on high 2 to 3 hours or until beans are
tender. Remove and discard ham bone. Puree beans, vegetables,
and liquid in food processor or electric blender in batches, filling
machine no more than ⅓ full with each batch. Correct seasoning
with salt and pepper. Add sherry. Return to slow-cooking pot.
Reheat and keep hot. Serve from the pot. *(See note on p. 14.)*
 • *Makes enough to serve 12 to 14.*

NOTE: A soup that takes well to garnishing, with sour cream, slices of avocado or hard-cooked egg, or paper-thin slices of lemon. All pretty and festive. Tastes good, too.

Portuguese Bean and Potato Soup

> 1 cup dried red beans
> 8 cups water
> 3 potatoes, peeled, diced
> 2 Tbs. tomato paste
> 1 (2-oz.) can anchovy fillets, drained, chopped
> Black pepper to taste

In slow-cooking pot, soak beans in water overnight. Cover and cook on high for 2 to 3 hours or until tender. Add remaining ingredients, cover and cook on low for 6 to 8 hours.

· *Makes 6 to 8 servings.*

MENU
SUGGESTION

Portuguese Bean and Potato Soup
Cucumber Sandwiches on Thin Rye Bread
Fresh Pineapple Sprinkled
with Coconut and Cognac
Coffee

White Bean Soup with Sour Cream

> 1 lb. dried white beans
> 8 cups water
> ¼ lb. uncooked ham, cut into small pieces
> 1 medium onion, peeled, chopped
> 1 bay leaf
> 1 tsp. salt
> Several grinds from peppermill
> ½ cup sour cream

In slow-cooking pot soak beans in water overnight; add remaining ingredients except sour cream. Cover and cook on low heat for 12 to 14 hours or until beans are soft. Remove bay leaf. Stir in sour cream just before serving. Serve very hot.

• *Makes 6 to 8 servings.*

MENU
SUGGESTION

White Bean Soup with Sour Cream
Red Caviar and Cream Cheese Sandwiches
on Dark Rye Bread
Dry White Wine
Bourbon Apples (see p. 156)

Pâtés

THE CLASSIC FRENCH pâté de foie gras, so often synonymous with the word pâté, is but one of hundreds of variations of pâté. Just about every small restaurant in France will have its own pâté maison, the favorite concoction of the owner-chef, and most French housewives will have their own pâté "specialty." Despite their glamorous connotations, pâtés are composed of readily available ingredients and, with the advent of the food processor, are childishly simple to make. We give you four versions, plus one made from delicatessen liverwurst that is fast, easy, and delicious; the others are more classic versions of what is in reality the most versatile of foods. Once you get used to making pâté you will probably go on to create your own versions.

The baked pâtés make a superb luncheon or supper entrée: add French potato salad, a few slices of tomato or cucumber, some crusty bread and a glass of red wine, and you have a feast. Or serve as the perfect appetizer with a touch of Dijon mustard and a few small sour pickles.

Now if you need further convincing, let me add that pâtés are supremely good for you with their high, vitamin-rich liver content, and of course they are top-quality protein as well. Last but not least, they are inexpensive. At this writing, less than six dollars' worth of ingredients made a baked pâté that provided twelve slices, enough for four as an entreé with ample leftover slices for a luncheon or appetizer serving.

Mixed Meat Pâté

> ½ lb. salt pork, in one thick piece
> 2 cloves garlic, peeled, quartered
> 1 medium onion, peeled, quartered
> 4 to 6 sprigs parsley
> ¼ tsp. crumbled thyme leaves
> 1 lb. lean beef, chilled until very firm, coarsely chopped
> 1 lb. lean veal, chilled until very firm, coarsely chopped
> ¼ lb. pork liver, chilled until very firm, coarsely chopped
> ½ cup soft bread crumbs
> 2 eggs
> ¼ cup brandy
> 1 tsp. coarsely ground black pepper
> ½ tsp. salt (or to taste)

Have the butcher cut the salt pork lengthwise into thin strips; place in a large pot and cover with water, bring to boil. Boil 1 minute, drain, blot dry. Line a 9¼ × 5¼ × 2¾-inch loaf pan with slightly overlapping strips of the blanched salt pork, using about ¾ of the strips. Set aside.

Put garlic and onion in work bowl of food processor, process until minced. Add parsley and thyme, process until minced. Start adding meats through feed tube, in order listed. Process until all meats are added and mixture is reduced to a puree. Add bread crumbs, process briefly. Add eggs, brandy, pepper, and salt, process until blended. Pour mixture into loaf pan over pork strips, spread out evenly. Cover completely with pork strips. Cover and seal pan with foil; with a small kitchen knife make 3 slits down center of foil to create air vents. Bake in a preheated 325° F. oven, for 2½ hours. Remove foil, cool. Place a clean sheet of foil directly on surface of pâté. Place a foil-covered brick (or similar weight) on top; refrigerate several hours or overnight. Unmold. To serve, cut in thin slices. *(See Menu Suggestion on p. 18.)*

> • *Makes about 12 servings.*

MENU
SUGGESTION

Mixed Meat Pâté
Corn on the Cob   Marinated Ripe Tomato Slices
French Bread
Imported Beer
Baked Lemon Pudding (see p. 162)

Pâté Diable

½ lb. salt pork, in one thick piece
1 clove garlic, peeled, minced *(optional)*
1 medium white onion, peeled, chopped
2 Tbs. butter
1 lb. lean veal, cut into cubes
1 lb. lean pork, cut into cubes
2 eggs
1½ tsp. salt
⅛ tsp. pepper
2 Tbs. Escoffier Sauce Diable
¼ cup brandy

Have your butcher cut the salt pork into thin slices, or do this yourself with food processor using thin-slicing disk; it will slice easily if very cold and firm but not frozen. Put the slices in a large skillet and cover with water, bring to a boil, boil 5 minutes; drain, pat dry, set aside (this step rids the pork of excess salt).

In a small skillet sauté the garlic and onion in the butter until tender; scrape contents of skillet into the work bowl of a food processor. Add meats and process until finely ground. Add remaining ingredients; process until mixture is very smooth.

Line the bottom and sides of a 9¼ × 5¼ × 2¾-inch loaf pan with strips of salt pork, using about ¾ of the strips. Pour in the pâté mixture; smooth out evenly with a spatula. Cover with remaining strips of salt pork. Cover and seal with aluminum foil, seal ends and sides of pan; place in a larger pan of boiling-hot water. Place in 300° F. oven, bake 1½ hours or until the pâté has shrunk slightly from the sides of the pan and the surrounding fat and juices are clear yellow with no traces of pink.

Remove the pan from the water and set it on a rack. Remove foil from pan and cover pâté directly with fresh foil; over this place a 3- to 4-lb. weight (I use a foil-wrapped clean brick). Cool at room temperature for several hours. Refrigerate until well chilled.

To serve, dip the bottom of the pan briefly in hot water, loosen sides of pâté from pan with a knife; unmold. Cut into thin slices.

• *Makes 8 to 10 servings.*

SUMMER-SUNDAY
SUPPER SUGGESTION

Pâté Diable
Cold Marinated Green Beans
Cherry Tomatoes
Pickles   Dijon Mustard
Hot French Rolls
Chilled Dry White Wine
Watermelon Slices

Ham Pâté

(For a buffet table)

A baked ham looks elegant on a buffet table and tastes elegant too, but so does ham pâté, which costs much less— not that you have to reveal this pleasant fact. Add potato salad, a tray of cucumber fingers, and hot rolls. Follow with Apricots Imperial (see p. 155) and coffee.

> 1½ lbs. canned ham, or use sufficient leftover baked or
>   boiled ham to make about 2½ cups finely chopped ham
> ½ cup sweet mixed pickles
> 1 Tbs. Dijon mustard
> 2 envelopes unflavored gelatin
> ½ cup dry white wine or water
> 2 Tbs. butter
> 1 Tbs. flour
> 1 cup chicken broth or stock, heated to boiling
> ½ cup milk, at room temperature

Coarsely chop ham, place in food processor with pickles and mustard; process until finely ground. Soften gelatin in wine, set aside. In saucepan melt butter, stir in flour; cook, stirring over low heat, 2 to 3 minutes. Add the boiling-hot stock, stir rapidly with whisk and cook until thickened. Stir in milk; add the softened gelatin and stir until dissolved. Cool slightly, add to ham mixture in processor; process until smooth and well blended. Pour into a 1-quart mold lightly greased with mayonnaise. Chill until firm. Unmold onto serving tray just before serving.
  • *Makes 8 to 10 servings.*

NOTE: Garnish platter, if you like, with crisp greens, but make them more interesting with the addition of fresh (or canned, if you must) pineapple cubes and pickled or brandied peach halves.

Pâté with Chicken Livers and Ham

½ lb. salt pork, in one thick piece
¾ lb. lean pork, cut into cubes
¾ lb. lean veal, cut into cubes
½ lb. calves' liver, cut into cubes
4 Tbs. butter
½ cup minced shallots or green onions
1 clove garlic, peeled, minced
⅓ lb. chicken livers
¼ cup cognac
1 egg
¼ tsp. allspice
1 tsp. salt
⅛ tsp. pepper
¼ lb. lean boiled ham, cut into ¼-inch cubes

Have your butcher cut the salt pork into thin slices, or do this yourself using a food processor with thin-slicing disk; it will slice easily if very cold and firm but not frozen. Put the slices in a large skillet and cover with water. Bring to a boil, boil 5 minutes; drain, blot dry, set aside (this step rids the pork of excess salt).

Put the pork, veal, and liver in the work bowl of a food processor; process until mixture is reduced to a smooth puree.

Melt 3 Tbs. of the butter in a small skillet; add the shallots and garlic, sauté until soft. Using a rubber spatula, scrape contents of skillet into processor work bowl over meats. Melt remaining butter in same skillet, add the chicken livers; cook, stirring often, until they are firm but still slightly pink in centers. Remove them with a slotted spoon and set aside. Pour the cognac into the hot skillet and boil it, stirring and scraping in any browned bits that cling to the bottom and sides of the pan, until cognac has reduced to about 2 Tbs. Pour this over the meats and shallots; add the egg and seasonings. Process until mixture is well blended. Remove the work bowl from processor base, gently lift out blade, then stir in ham cubes.

Line the bottom and sides of a 1½-quart mold or loaf pan with strips of salt pork; pour in half of the pâté mixture, pressing it down firmly. Cut the chicken livers in quarters or halves depending on size and lay them in a row down the center of the pâté. Cover with remaining pâté mixture; gently press down and spread out evenly. Cover and seal the mold with foil; place it in a large pan of hot water. Bake in preheated 300° F. oven for 2 hours or until pâté shrinks slightly from sides of mold. Remove from hot water to a rack; remove foil from mold. Cover pâté directly with fresh foil; place a 2 to 2½-lb. weight over the foil (a foil-covered brick, or a heavy pan, casserole, or other weight that will fit into the mold). Let stand at room temperature for several hours, then refrigerate until well chilled. Unmold by dipping the bottom of the mold briefly into hot water; loosen sides with a knife, invert onto serving plate. Cut into thin slices.

• *Makes 8 to 10 servings.*

MENU
SUGGESTION

Platter of Pâté and Melon Slices
Steamed new potatoes (the smallest you can find),
served in their jackets
Hot Buttered French Rolls
Chilled Beaujolais
Chocolate Strawberries (see p. 161)

★

After-Work Pâté Maison

1 lb. top-quality liverwurst, at room temperature
½ cup (1 stick) butter, at room temperature
2 Tbs. cognac
2 Tbs. Escoffier Sauce Diable
1 tsp. Dijon mustard
Salt
Pepper

Combine ingredients, blend until smooth. Season with salt and pepper. Place in a small crock. Chill. Turn out or serve from the crock.

NOTE: Devastating as double martinis, this pâté is best when served with very thin slices of French-style bread cut from a long thin loaf.

COCKTAIL PARTY
SUGGESTION

After-Work Pâté Maison
Thin-Sliced Rye Bread
Red Caviar-stuffed Eggs
Big English Pickled Onions
Bowl of Walnut Halves and Raisins

Sandwiches

A SANDWICH, of course, is some sort of filling between two layers of bread, but did you ever stop to think that the "bread" need not be just plain old sliced bread? The "bread" can be delicate crepes folded over all manner of fillings, or it can be Greek pita bread, the "pocket" filled with spicy meat; the great American hamburger will taste even greater on an English muffin. Come to think of it, a Mexican tortilla is bread too: tortillas turned into enchiladas and tostadas are sandwiches in the grand sense. Then there are crusty hard rolls for the beloved heroes and "po' boys." If the sandwich does call for just bread, there is an endless variety to choose from: French loaves, homemade whole wheat, light and dark rye, pumpernickel, and of course firm, honest white. The point is, a sandwich can be an adventure in eating, and the right sandwich can indeed make a meal.

And that's just what sandwiches are now: meal size. Add a bowl of iced raw vegetables if you like, a glass of wine or perhaps cold beer, or just plenty of fresh hot coffee. Desserts to follow sandwiches are easy. Best of all is fresh fruit, whatever is ripe and beautiful: peaches, all sorts of melon, watermelon (perfect for a summer day), fragrant yellow pears, grapes, tangerines; all of them make a great ending for a sandwich meal.

For a party you can assemble several different kinds of fillings. Have a tray of breads, any type that suits the fillings; add fruit and coffee, and the party takes care of itself. People love sandwiches; they are a great way to entertain and they are also a great answer for a delicious lunch or supper. Perfect, too, for our favorite porch or fireside meals. Served where we like as well as

when we like, the great American sandwich is indeed an answer
meal and a favorite one.

Greek Gyro

*In Greek or Near East restaurants this sandwich is made
with well-seasoned lamb that is cooked on a slowly rotating
vertical spit. As the outer surface of the meat browns it is
sliced off and popped into pita bread "pockets." You can use
leftover roast lamb or, as in this version, ground-lamb
patties.*

2 slices whole wheat bread
1 clove garlic, peeled
2 sprigs parsley
1 lb. lean lamb, cut into 1-inch cubes
½ tsp. salt
1 tsp. chili powder
½ tsp. ground cumin
1 small white onion, peeled, chopped
½ cup sour cream
½ tsp. salt
½ tsp. dried dill
1 Tbs. lemon juice
1 medium tomato
4 pita rolls
2 cups shredded lettuce

In work bowl of food processor process bread to fine crumbs;
remove from bowl, set aside. Turn on processor and, while
motor is running, drop garlic through feed tube into processor
bowl; process until finely chopped, add parsley and process until
minced. Add lamb cubes, process until lamb is finely ground;
add salt, chili powder, cumin, and bread crumbs; process briefly
to mix ingredients. Remove and shape mixture into four patties.
   Combine chopped onion, sour cream, salt, dill, and lemon
juice. Cut tomato in half, gently squeeze out seeds and juice, cut
halves into strips, add to sour-cream mixture.

Broil lamb patties, preferably on outdoor grill over glowing coals.

Heat pita rolls. Cut or split in half horizontally; place a broiled lamb patty on bottom half. Top with a spoonful of the sour-cream mixture, add shredded lettuce, more sour-cream mixture, and top half of roll.

• *Makes 4 sandwiches.*

NOTE: To prepare lamb patties by hand, have your butcher grind the lamb. Make bread crumbs in an electric blender or use packaged bread crumbs. Mince garlic and parsley. Combine lamb, bread crumbs, and seasonings and blend well; form into patties.

★

Pan Bagna

This French version of an Italian hero is great for picnics: on the beach, in the park, or before the TV. The name means, literally, "bathed bread," since the bread is bathed in a flavorful vinaigrette dressing.

Water
1 medium green pepper, halved, seeded, cut into strips
4 hard-crusted French rolls or hero rolls
Vinaigrette dressing (*see below*)
2 medium tomatoes, thinly sliced, slices cut in half
4 hard-cooked eggs, sliced
1 (2-oz.) can flat anchovy fillets, drained
1 cup shredded lettuce
12 pitted ripe olives, sliced

★

Vinaigrette dressing

1 clove garlic, peeled, minced
½ cup mild oil
2 Tbs. red wine vinegar
½ tsp. sugar
¼ tsp. salt

Several grinds from peppermill (filled with black Java
   peppercorns)
¼ tsp. leaf basil, crumbled

Combine ingredients for vinaigrette dressing; set aside to mellow.
   In a small saucepan cover green-pepper strips with water,
bring to boil, boil 1 minute; drain, set aside.
   Cut rolls in half horizontally, drizzle about 1 Tbs. vinaigrette
dressing on each cut side. Arrange tomato slices on bottom
halves of rolls, overlapping to fit; top with green-pepper strips,
hard-cooked egg slices, anchovy fillets, shredded lettuce, and
olive slices. Cover with top halves of rolls; press down gently to
hold sandwiches together.
   • *Makes 4 sandwiches.*

Mexican Hot Dogs

A scrumptious sandwich to serve with cold beer!

2 Tbs. butter
1 medium onion, peeled and minced
1 (8-oz.) can Mexican refried beans
8 frankfurters
8 tortillas
1 (4-oz.) can enchilada sauce
1 large avocado, peeled and chopped
1 small head lettuce, shredded
1 large tomato, peeled, seeded, and cut into strips
Shredded cheddar cheese

Melt butter in a heavy skillet, sauté onion in butter until soft.
Add beans, cook over medium heat until very hot. Split and broil
frankfurters. Heat tortillas in a medium oven. Heat enchilada
sauce in a small saucepan. Spread tortillas with bean mixture, add
frankfurters; place on serving plate. Cover with enchilada sauce.
Top with avocado, lettuce, and tomato. Sprinkle heavily with
cheese. Serve very hot.
   • *Makes 4 servings of 2 each (maybe only 2 servings, they
   are so good).*

California Hero

So good, it's only incidental that it's so good for you.

2 (4-oz.) packages alfalfa sprouts (total 1 cup)
2 Tbs. mild salad oil
2 Tbs. lemon juice
½ tsp. salt
2–3 grinds from peppermill
1 large round loaf sourdough bread, about 9 inches
   in diameter
1 large avocado, peeled, pitted, and sliced
¼ lb. thinly sliced Genoa salami
½ lb. provolone cheese, cut into 8 thin slices

Mix together sprouts, oil, lemon juice, salt and pepper. Cut off top half of bread; scoop out center, leaving a shell about 1 inch thick (reserve inside for crumbs to use in another recipe).

Place sprout mixture on bottom half of bread, cover with avocado slices, salami, and cheese. Replace top of bread. Cut into wedges to serve.
   • *Makes 6 servings.*

Lamb-Stuffed Pitas

Pita bread has become a great favorite; here is a trio of ways to stuff it for an interesting and complete meal.

1 clove garlic, peeled, minced
½ cup thinly sliced celery
½ cup chopped onion
½ cup chopped green pepper
2 small yellow squash, thinly sliced
¼ cup mild oil
2 Tbs. butter
½ lb. lean lamb, ground
½ cup raisins

½ cup pine nuts
1 cup tomato sauce, homemade or canned
½ tsp. oregano
Salt
Pepper
6 pita rolls
6 thin slices Havarti cheese (or other mild mellow cheese)

Sauté garlic, celery, onion, green pepper, and squash in oil and butter over low heat until vegetables are tender but still slightly crisp. In second skillet, sauté lamb until no longer pink. Add raisins, pine nuts, and sautéed vegetables. Add tomato sauce and oregano; simmer, stirring often, until flavors blend, about 10 minutes. Season with salt and pepper. Heat pita rolls in 350° F. oven; split open, but not apart; fill with lamb mixture, place on baking sheet. Top each filled pita with a slice of cheese, place in 350° F. oven until cheese melts.

Oriental Pita Burgers

1 lb. lean beef, ground
1 large onion peeled, chopped
1 Tbs. oil
1 (10-oz.) package frozen Chinese vegetables
¼ cup water
½ cup fresh bean sprouts
Soy sauce
4 pita rolls

Sauté ground beef and onion in oil over medium heat until meat is no longer pink. Add frozen Chinese vegetables and water. Stir, then cover and steam 5 minutes or until vegetables are tender but still slightly crisp. Uncover; cook, stirring, until all liquid has evaporated. Stir in bean sprouts; season liberally with soy sauce. Heat pita rolls, split, and fill pockets with meat mixture. Serve at once.
   • *Makes 4 servings.*

Cheeseburger Pitas

1 lb. lean beef, ground
1 Tbs. butter
½ tsp. salt
1 tsp. Worcestershire sauce
2 Tbs. catsup
1 tsp. Dijon mustard
1 large tomato, cut into wedges
1 small mild purple onion, peeled, chopped
¼ lb. crumbled sharp cheddar cheese
4 pita rolls

Sauté beef in butter until no longer pink; stir in next 7 ingredients, stir until heated, keep hot. Heat pita rolls in 350° F. oven; split, fill with hot meat mixture. Serve at once.
 • *Makes 4 servings.*

West Coast Burger

This is my all-time favorite sandwich. A meal in itself, it needs only a glass of good red wine or cold beer.

¼ cup Worcestershire sauce
2 Tbs. catsup
Juice from 1 lemon
Dash Tabasco sauce
2–3 grinds from peppermill
Salt
1 lb. lean beef, ground
2 split and toasted English muffins
2 Tbs. butter, at room temperature
1 medium tomato, sliced
1 medium avocado, peeled, seeded, sliced
2 cups shredded lettuce
1 cup shredded cheddar cheese

In a small pitcher combine Worcestershire sauce, catsup, lemon juice, Tabasco, pepper, and salt to taste. Stir to a blended sauce.

Divide meat into 4 patties. Broil (preferably over glowing coals) until medium rare. Spread toasted (still warm) halves of English muffins with butter; place each half on a serving plate. Top with broiled meat patty, one-fourth of tomato slices, avocado slices, shredded lettuce, and cheese.

Stir sauce to reblend; pour equally over hamburgers.

• *Makes 4 burgers.*

A Different Ham and Cheese

A great sandwich to serve with an assortment of fresh fruit; melon and peach slices would be lovely.

8 slices firm white bread
Smithfield ham spread
Sharp cheddar cheese spread
3 large eggs
3 tbs. milk
Butter, about 4 Tbs.
Crisp sweet pickles

Trim crusts from bread. Spread 4 slices with a thin covering of Smithfield ham spread, then a thick layer of cheddar cheese spread. Cover with remaining bread slices. Beat eggs and milk together in a small bowl just until blended. Pour mixture into a pie plate. Dip sandwiches on both sides.

Melt about 2 Tbs. of the butter on an electric grill or in a large skillet. Sauté sandwiches, turning once, until golden. Add more butter as needed. Serve with crisp sweet pickles.

• *Makes 4 sandwiches.*

Crepes

WHEN MOST PEOPLE THINK "CREPES," they also think "French"; but crepes are by no means an exclusively French creation. There are Russian blini, Jewish blintz; even the Mexican enchilada is, in reality, a crepe that is made with mesa meal instead of flour. The French word *crepe* literally means very thin pancake.

Basic crepes are so easy you will probably find endless ways to serve them as entrées as well as desserts. They are the perfect answer, an elegant and easy answer, to the search for delicious, satisfying, yet lighter food that has led to our revolution against heavy-handed meals that offer little except extra calories.

Crepes too are yet another version of our new liking for one-dish meals. Served with any number of fillings, they need little else but a garnish on the plate to complete a perfect lunch or supper.

We offer you here six main-dish fillings, but I am sure they will mark only the beginning of your crepe repertoire once you start serving crepes.

Basic Crepes

4 eggs
¼ tsp. salt
2 cups unbleached flour
1 cup milk
½ cup water
2 Tbs. cognac, brandy, or applejack, or substitute
    2 more Tbs. water
2 Tbs. butter

To prepare Basic Crepes:

ELECTRIC MIXER OR WHISK METHOD: In medium bowl beat eggs, add flour and milk alternately, beating after each addition; beat in water, brandy, and butter.

BLENDER METHOD: Combine ⅓ of all ingredients in blender jar, blend about 1 minute. Use rubber spatula to scrape down sides of bowl, blend 30 seconds. Repeat with remaining ingredients.

PROCESSOR METHOD: Combine ingredients in work bowl of processor. Process until smooth, about 30 seconds.

WHICHEVER METHOD USED: Refrigerate batter 1 hour (or longer) before making crepes.

To make crepes: Use a 6- to 8-inch crepe pan (or substitute any low-sided omelet or similar pan). Put about 1 tsp. butter in pan; swirl until pan is completely coated, add about 1½ Tbs. batter; tilt pan until bottom is covered. Cook about ½ minute, turn with spatula, cook ½ minute. Remove from pan and repeat until all batter is used.

If you prefer a thinner crepe, add more milk. A crisper crepe? Substitute ½ cup water for equivalent of milk.

If making ahead, stack with waxed paper between each crepe, wrap stack in foil, and store in freezer. Thaw at room temperature.

Crespoleni

A glass of Chianti makes this the perfect one-dish luncheon or supper.

> 2 (10-oz.) packages frozen chopped spinach, thawed and drained, or 1½ lbs. fresh spinach, steamed, drained, and chopped
> 1 cup small-curd cottage cheese
> ½ cup grated Parmesan cheese
> 2 eggs
> ¼ tsp. salt
> 16 crepes *(see p. 33)*
> 3 cups Italian-style tomato sauce *(see p. 133)*
> ¼ cup more cottage cheese

Blot cooked chopped spinach dry with paper toweling. Put in work bowl of food processor; process to a puree. Add cottage cheese, Parmesan cheese, eggs, and salt. Process briefly to blend; spoon about 2 Tbs. mixture into center of each cooked crepe. Roll up; place in shallow baking dish. Pour tomato sauce over filled crepes, sprinkle with the ¼ cup cottage cheese. Bake in pre-heated 350° F. conventional oven for 20 to 30 minutes, in convection oven at 300° F. for 15 to 20 minutes, in microwave oven 5 to 8 minutes.

> • *Makes 16 crepes.*

Dairy Special Crepes

A lovely summer lunch (or late breakfast). Serve with plenty of hot, fresh coffee.

> 1 (8-oz.) package cream cheese, at room temperature
> ½ cup sour cream
> 1 (8-oz.) can crushed pineapple, well drained
> 1 (3½-oz.) package chopped walnuts
> 8 crepes *(see p. 33)*
> Chopped walnuts

Combine cream cheese, sour cream, pineapple, and walnuts. Fill center of crepes with mixture, fold over, decorate with a sprinkle of chopped walnuts. Serve lightly chilled.

• *Makes 4 servings.*

Shrimp Creole Crepes

Serve with a glass of dry, chilled white wine. Dessert could be orange slices with coconut.

3 slices bacon
2 Tbs. minced green onion
2 Tbs. minced green pepper
1 (1-lb.) can Italian-style tomatoes with basil
½ cup dry white wine
2–3 dashes Tabasco sauce
Salt
1 lb. raw shrimp, shelled, deveined
Freshly ground black pepper
8 crepes *(see p. 33)*

Cook the bacon in a large heavy skillet over very low heat until crisp. Remove, drain, crumble, and reserve. Sauté the onions and green pepper in the rendered fat until limp. Add tomatoes, wine, Tabasco, pepper, and salt. Simmer over low heat for 20 to 30 minutes. Add shrimp, cook only until shrimp are pink, 5 to 10 minutes. Heat crepes briefly in oven. Spoon shrimp mixture onto heated crepes, fold over, sprinkle with reserved crumbled bacon. Serve hot.

• *Makes 4 servings.*

Crab Crepes Imperial

This is the ultimate in crepery, good enough to serve at a wedding breakfast or the next time you have Queen Elizabeth over to lunch.

1 cup cooked crabmeat, fresh or frozen
3 Tbs. butter
3 Tbs. flour
1 cup milk
½ cup dry white wine
½ cup grated Gruyère cheese
½ cup toasted slivered almonds
8 cooked crepes *(see p. 33)*
Finely chopped parsley

Drain and flake crabmeat. Helt butter in a heavy skillet, stir in flour; cook, stirring, 2 or 3 minutes over low heat. Add milk and wine, blend to a smooth sauce. Cook, stirring, until thick. Add cheese and continue to cook until cheese melts. Add crabmeat and almonds. Cook until very hot. Spoon mixture onto ½ of each crepe, fold over, sprinkle with parsley, and serve at once.
• *Makes 4 servings.*

MENU
SUGGESTION

Crab Crepes Imperial
Steamed Fresh Asparagus
Frozen Cream Puffs Filled with Cognac-
flavored Whipped Cream
Fresh or Frozen Raspberries
Champagne

Chicken and Broccoli Crepes Mornay*

4 Tbs. butter
4 Tbs. flour
2 cups chicken stock or broth, heated to boiling
Dash Tabasco sauce
¼ tsp. salt
1 egg yolk
½ cup heavy cream
¼ cup grated Swiss cheese
1 cup cooked diced chicken
1 (10-oz.) package frozen broccoli or ¾ lb. fresh broccoli,
    cooked, drained, and chopped
8 crepes *(see p. 33)*
¼ cup more grated Swiss cheese

Melt butter in saucepan. Blend in flour; add boiling-hot stock and stir rapidly with whisk until thick and smooth. Remove from heat, season with Tabasco sauce and salt. Mix egg yolk with cream. Stir small amount of hot mixture into egg mixture, then stir egg mixture into saucepan. Add ¼ cup cheese; cook, stirring over low heat, one minute. Stir in chicken and broccoli. In large shallow baking dish, fill crepes with chicken mixture; or arrange in individual baking dishes. Fold over. Sprinkle with remaining cheese. Cover and heat in conventional 350° F. oven for 15 to 20 minutes, in convection oven at 250° F. for 10 to 15 minutes, or in microwave oven until heated, about 5 minutes.
  • *Makes 8 filled crepes (4 servings).*

*This extra-special crepe dish can be served with same menu suggested for Crab Crepes Imperial on previous page.

Ham and Cheese Crepes

16 thin slices baked ham
16 thin slices Gruyère cheese
16 crepes *(see p. 33)*
½ pt. sour cream
Grated Parmesan cheese
Paprika

Place a slice of ham and one of cheese on each crepe and roll up.
Arrange in a long, shallow casserole, or place 4 crepes in each of
4 individual casserole dishes. Spoon sour cream over crepes.
Sprinkle with Parmesan cheese and paprika. Place in preheated
350° F. conventional oven, in convection oven at 250° F., or in
microwave oven until bubbly hot.
   • *Makes 4 servings.*

FESTIVE LUNCHEON
SUGGESTION

Ham and Cheese Crepes
Bibb Lettuce with Poppy Seed Dressing
Chilled Champagne
Lemon Ice Cream (see p. 165)
with Fresh or Frozen Blueberries

Salads, Salad Dressings, and Antipastos

THE KITCHEN REVOLUTION has produced a new main dish—the salad. Our interest in lighter "vitality" foods has started a completely new direction for what used to be a pallid accompaniment but is now instead the star attraction—the epicure's salad. For these are no ordinary lettuce-and-tomato side dishes. These are robust, substantial meals in themselves, needing only the addition of interesting bread, some wine perhaps, and for those with an insatiable sweet tooth, a good dessert.

The new cuisine naturally calls for easy, quick-to-prepare meals, and what could be simpler than a great salad? The secret to success at the table lies not in complicated preparation but in the selection of ingredients. New to most tables today is an endless variety of greens: lettuce is no longer just lettuce but romaine, Bibb, and Boston, to name only a few. Iceberg lettuce, that old familiar standby, is still with us, but now it is served finely shredded or in crisp wedges rather than torn into bite-size pieces; the Boston variety is best for that, while romaine takes kindly to shredding. As for Bibb, that queen of the lettuce patch, it should merely be separated into leaves and enjoyed.

But lettuce is only one type of greenery. Spinach too has become a favorite, along with watercress, Italian rugola, Chinese cabbage, and parsley. This last is now finely minced and added in generous measure any time extra greenery and vitamins are wanted. It's distinctly "old hat" to use it for a never-eaten garnish.

Newest of all salad ingredients are sprouts, to add great-tasting crunch to just about any salad going, plus packing a powerhouse of vitamins. Sprouts are easy and quick to grow.

All that's needed is a mason jar, a piece of cheesecloth, and an elastic band, plus your choice of seeds. The seeds are simply rinsed well, then placed in the jar, covered with tepid water, and stored overnight in a dark place. Cover the top of the jar with the cheesecloth and secure with the elastic band. Place in a fairly warm dark place—under the sink is perfect. Drain, rinse (the cheesecloth keeps the seeds from falling out of the jar), re-store. The seeds should then be rinsed two or three times a day, drained well, and returned to the dark. Sprouting takes place in two or three days. Favorite seeds for sprouting are mung beans, soybeans, and cress, but any health-food store can fill you in on other varieties if you want to be adventurous.

Most salad greenery is fragile and needs a little care in handling. For the freshest and crispest, it's best to buy it fresh to start with. Take the trouble to find out which days your market receives fresh produce, and shop early in the day. A tactful request plus a small tip will usually get you in the back wrapping room, where you can get the more perishable greens before they are inevitably sealed in plastic—a regrettable practice beloved of supermarkets but death on crisp greenery. If you can manage this, ask the "boys in the back room" to wrap your purchases in wet paper towels, and don't let the packer at the checkout counter put the canned tomatoes on top of the watercress—a procedure they seem to love.

You can of course get superior local produce at roadside stands or farmers' markets in season, but don't fall for those markets that feature tomatoes in March or corn in April. What they are selling is second-rate shipped-in produce already rejected by the supermarkets. Buy local produce, in season only, and look before you buy; those homespun boys in denim are not always just "good ole dirt farmers." If in doubt you are better off in a reputable supermarket.

SALADS

White Bean Salad with Anchovies and Greek Olives

Make a meal with this salad; add some sliced tomatoes and cucumbers. A good imported beer is perfect here.

1 small can anchovy fillets
2 Tbs. salad oil
2 Tbs. white wine vinegar
Freshly ground black pepper
3 cups hot, cooked white beans
2 large green onions, minced
3 or 4 stalks celery, thinly sliced
Greek olives
Lemon wedges

Drain oil from anchovy fillets into a large bowl, chop anchovies, set aside. Add salad oil and vinegar to bowl plus a sprinkling of pepper; beat with a fork or small whisk until blended. Add hot beans, green onion, and chopped anchovy fillets. Stir gently with a large spoon until beans are coated with dressing. Let salad stand at room temperature for 30 minutes to 1 hour (not absolutely essential, but this standing allows the flavor of the dressing to be absorbed by the beans). Add celery, toss lightly. Serve the salad garnished with black olives. Add a lemon wedge to each serving.

• *Makes about 6 servings.*

Greek Salad Deluxe

Cold imported beer is a great beverage for this salad; for bread, try splitting and toasting pita rolls. Add a dessert, say, the stuffed dates on page 162, and finish with small cups of very black coffee.

2 heads Boston lettuce, trimmed, torn into bite-size pieces
1 head romaine lettuce, trimmed, thinly shredded
4 tomatoes, quartered
2 cucumbers, peeled, thinly sliced
12 to 18 Greek olives (available in jars)
16 to 24 stuffed grape leaves (available in jars)
12 large pickled onions (available in jars)
½ lb. feta cheese, crumbled
½ cup vinaigrette dressing (see p. 55)
1 tsp. dried oregano

Combine Boston and romaine lettuce in salad bowl. Arrange tomatoes, cucumbers, stuffed grape leaves, and pickled onions in an attractive design over lettuce. Sprinkle with crumbled cheese. Bring salad and vinaigrette dressing to the table separately. Just before serving, add dressing and oregano to salad. Toss briefly and serve.

• *Makes 4 to 6 servings.*

★

Rice Salad

4 cups chilled cooked rice
1 cup chilled cooked peas
1 cup finely chopped lean baked or boiled ham
½ cup finely chopped celery
½ cup chopped Major Gray chutney
1 Tbs. salad oil
1 cup mayonnaise (or ½ cup mayonnaise,
    ½ cup sour cream)
Salt
Freshly ground black pepper

Combine ingredients, toss with a fork to mix. Season to taste with salt and pepper. Refrigerate several hours so that flavors blend.

• *Makes about 8 servings.*

NOTE: Omit chopped ham; instead spoon salad onto thin slices of ham, roll up, and serve on slices of pineapple. Garnish ham rolls with a bit of mayonnaise or sour cream. Or for a truly special salad add ½ lb. cooked, shelled, and deveined chopped shrimp.

MENU
SUGGESTION

Rice Salad
Whole-wheat Bread-and-butter Sandwiches
Fresh Peaches with Cognac
Coffee

Kidney Bean and Frankfurter Salad

*A great picnic salad; serve with rye-bread-and-butter sand-
wiches and cherry tomatoes. Add a super dessert, say,
Peanut Butter Cake, and plenty of coffee for a great finish.*

6 frankfurters
1 Tbs. sugar
1 tsp. salt
¼ tsp. coarsely ground black pepper
2 Tbs. cider vinegar
½ cup salad oil
¼ cup chopped crisp sweet pickles
¼ cup minced chives or green onion
2 cups cooked red kidney beans or
    1 (1-lb.) can kidney beans, drained
2 cups shredded iceberg lettuce

Place frankfurters in shallow skillet, cover with water, bring to
a boil; simmer 2 to 3 minutes. Drain, cool slightly, cut into
½-inch slices. Set aside.

In small bowl combine sugar, salt, pepper, vinegar, and oil;
beat with whisk until sugar has dissolved. Or place ingredients
in electric blender or food processor; blend or process until sugar
dissolves. Add pickles and chives. Pour mixture over beans in
a salad bowl. Add frankfurters, toss to blend. Cover and refrigerate several hours. Just before serving add lettuce; toss
lightly.

   • *Makes 4 to 6 servings.*

Chicken Salad with Grapes

Meat from 2½- to 3-lb. poached chicken, skinned, boned, and cut into bite-size pieces.
6 to 8 stalks celery, thinly sliced
2 or 3 medium-size tart apples, peeled, cored, and chopped
1 (small) package slivered almonds
½ to 1 cup seedless white grapes
¾ to 1 cup homemade mayonnaise *(see p. 57)*
1 Tbs. lemon juice
Salt to taste

Combine ingredients, blend well. Cover and refrigerate several hours to allow flavors to mellow and blend.
• *Makes 4 to 6 servings.*

MENU
SUGGESTION

*Chicken Salad
with Grapes
Hot Buttered Rolls
Poppy-Seed Cake* (see p. 147)
Coffee

Fisherman's Salad

2 lbs. poached fish fillets *(see basic recipe opposite page)*
¼ cup finely chopped green onion
½ cup chopped celery
¼ cup finely chopped green pepper
1 (small) jar chopped pimientos, drained
½ cup salad oil
¼ cup wine vinegar
1 tsp. salt
¼ tsp. coarsely ground black pepper

¼ tsp. dry mustard
¼ cup sour cream
¼ cup mayonnaise
¼ cup minced parsley
Salt to taste
Salad greens
Paprika

Cut still-warm poached fish fillets into small pieces. Put in a bowl; add all ingredients except sour cream, mayonnaise, and minced parsley; toss gently. Refrigerate several hours to chill salad and mellow flavors. Pour off and discard any dressing not absorbed by salad ingredients. Add mayonnaise, sour cream, and parsley; toss gently. Serve on lettuce leaves. Sprinkle with paprika.

   • *Makes about 4 cups salad.*

Easy Basic Poached Fillet of Fish

1 cup bottled clam juice
3 cups water
½ to 1 cup dry white wine
1 small onion, peeled and quartered
1 small carrot, scraped and sliced
1 stalk celery, sliced
4 to 6 white peppercorns
1 bay leaf
Parsley sprig
2 lbs. fresh fish fillets

Combine all ingredients except fish fillets in a large (10-inch) skillet. Let simmer over low heat about 30 minutes. Remove vegetables, peppercorns, bay leaf, and parsley with a slotted spoon. Gently lower fish into barely simmering liquid. Do not crowd skillet; poach only a few fillets at a time.

Using a spatula, gently remove fillets from pan as soon as flesh turns white and firm. Cooking time should be no more than 5 minutes. Place poached fillets in a single layer in a long shallow glass baking dish or on a platter. Cover with plastic wrap, and refrigerate until ready to use in salad.

- *Makes 2½ to 3 cups loosely packed flaked fish for salads or other cold or hot dishes.*

MENU
SUGGESTION

Fisherman's Salad
French Bread and Butter
Tropical Pineapple Cake (see p. 145)
Coffee

Crabmeat Salad

½ lb. poached fish fillets *(see basic recipe, p. 45)*
1 lb. crabmeat
4 stalks celery, very thinly sliced (about 1 cup)
2 Tbs. lemon juice
4 Tbs. mayonnaise (preferably homemade; *see p. 57*)
Salt
1 Tbs. capers

Flake fish fillets. Remove cartilage from crabmeat. Combine all ingredients, blending well. Refrigerate several hours to mellow flavors.

- *Makes about 3 cups salad.*

NOTE: You can "extend" this salad by serving it in avocado halves or tomato shells on lettuce-lined plates, or in the center of a tomato aspic ring. It's also just scrumptious served very cold on buttered and toasted rolls.

MENU
SUGGESTION

Crabmeat Salad
Sliced Tomatoes
Corn Sticks
Banana Rum Sorbet (see p. 167)
Coffee

Salade Niçoise

There are as many variations of this classic salad from the French Riviera as there are recipes for fruitcake, but this comes closest to being the "real thing." Serve it as it would be served in Nice, preferably outdoors on a sunny terrace, accompanied by real French bread and a light fruity Beaujolais; follow with fruit and cheese for dessert.

2 lbs. small new potatoes
½ cup salad oil
¼ cup white wine vinegar
¼ cup dry white wine
½ tsp. black pepper
¼ tsp salt
1½ lbs. green beans
4 stalks celery, chopped
Lettuce leaves
1 (7½-oz.) can tuna fish
1 (2½-oz.) can anchovies
1 large ripe tomato, peeled and quartered
8 to 12 large ripe olives

Steam the new potatoes on a rack over boiling water in a covered pot until tender. Drain, cut in quarters, and place in a large bowl. Combine oil, vinegar, wine, pepper, and salt. Beat well with a fork. Pour over still-warm potatoes. Steam green beans until tender; add beans and celery to potatoes. Mix with a fork. Refrigerate at least 4 hours. Just before serving, pile potato-bean mixture onto lettuce leaves on plates. Garnish with chunks of tuna, anchovies, tomato quarters, and olives.

• *Makes 4 servings.*

Classic Caesar Salad

The perfect meal salad; serve with toasted rolls that have first been split, buttered, and liberally sprinkled with Parmesan cheese. A red wine suits a Caesar best, perhaps a good Chianti. For dessert, try soaking pound cake in rum and adding a little whipped cream and toasted almonds to each serving. Small cups of espresso make a perfect finale.

> 2 head romaine lettuce, washed, chilled, and torn into
>   bite-size pieces
> ¼ cup salad oil
> Juice of 1 large lemon
> ¼ tsp. dry mustard
> ¼ tsp. pepper
> ½ cup grated Parmesan cheese
> 2 eggs
> 2 cups crisp croutons
> 1 (2½-oz.) can anchovies, drained
> 6 slices crisp bacon, crumbled *(optional)*

Place the lettuce in a large salad bowl. Combine oil, lemon juice, mustard, and pepper; blend well, pour over lettuce. Add Parmesan cheese, toss lightly to blend. Break eggs over salad, toss thoroughly with a fork until greens are lightly coated and no trace of egg remains. Sprinkle with croutons, toss again. Garnish with anchovies and crumbled bacon.

• *Makes 4 to 6 servings.*

Ham and Potato Salad with Bean Sprouts

    3 lbs. small new potatoes
    1 cup mayonnaise
    ¼ cup soy sauce
    ¼ cup white wine vinegar
    1 cup fresh bean sprouts
    1 large red pepper, minced
    1½ cups diced ham

Steam the new potatoes on a rack over boiling water in a covered pot until just tender; drain, cut in halves or quarters, place in a large salad bowl. Add mayonnaise, soy sauce, and vinegar; mix gently with a fork. Refrigerate at least 4 hours. About 1 hour before serving, add remaining ingredients, toss to blend.
    • *Makes 4 to 6 servings.*

MENU
SUGGESTION

*Ham and Potato Salad
with Bean Sprouts
Split and Toasted Rolls
Beaujolais
Orange Slices with Grand Marnier
and Grated Coconut*

Blue Cheese Potato Salad with Avocado Slices

Another hearty potato salad that makes a meal; nice to serve with slices of cold pâté or deli meats. Add some sliced tomatoes, a fruit dessert, and coffee for a great lunch or supper. If you want to serve wine, a California Cabernet-Sauvignon is perfect.

2½ lbs. small new potatoes
½ cup minced parsley
½ cup minced green onions
½ cup salad oil
¼ cup wine vinegar
1 tsp. sugar
½ tsp. pepper
¼ tsp. salt
1 cup crumbled blue cheese
1 large avocado, peeled, sliced

Steam the new potatoes on a rack over boiling water in a covered pot until tender. Drain, cut in halves or quarters. Combine with parsley and green onion in a large bowl. Combine salad oil, vinegar, sugar, pepper, and salt in a small bowl. Beat with a whisk until thick and sugar is thoroughly dissolved. Pour over still-warm potato mixture.

Refrigerate at least 4 hours. Sprinkle with blue cheese and toss with a fork, let stand at room temperature for an hour before serving. Garnish with avocado slices.

• *Makes 4 to 6 servings.*

Green Bean and Potato Salad

This is summer fare, for the dish depends on the availability of small, fresh, new potatoes and equally fresh green beans. These ingredients may be found, with a little searching, in supermarkets and of course at good roadside produce stands. It makes a fabulous warm-weather supper served with mustard-packed sardines, crusty bread, and a glass of Beaujolais. Wind up with fresh blueberries or peaches enhanced with a little sour cream and a dusting of brown sugar.

1 tsp. sugar
3 Tbs. white wine vinegar
¾ cup salad oil
½ tsp. salt
½ tsp. coarsely ground black pepper
2 Tbs. chopped fresh basil *(optional)*
3 lbs. small new potatoes
1½ lbs. fresh green beans
½ cup dry white wine

Dissolve sugar in vinegar in a small bowl. Add salad oil, salt, and pepper, beat with a fork until well blended. Stir in basil, set aside. Place new potatoes on a rack set over boiling water, cover, and steam until tender; the time depends on the size of the potatoes. Drain, cut in quarters (or halves if very small), place in large salad bowl while still hot. Reblend dressing, pour over potatoes. Refrigerate at least 4 hours. Trim green beans, steam until tender-crisp. Tarnsfer to a nonmetal bowl, add wine, lifting and turning to blend. Refrigerate 3 to 4 hours. To serve, drain green beans, add to potatoes, lift and toss to blend. Allow salad to come to room temperature before serving.

• *Makes 6 servings.*

Salade à la Russe

> 1 cup homemade mayonnaise *(see p. 57)*
> ⅓ cup catsup
> 2 Tbs. (bottled) horseradish
> 1 Tbs. white wine vinegar
> 1 Tbs. strained lemon juice
> 3 dashes Tabasco sauce
> 1 tsp. Worcestershire sauce
> 1 Tbs. grated onion
> 1 (2-oz.) jar caviar
> 8 firm wedges (¼ head each) lettuce
> 8 hard-cooked eggs, shelled, chilled, and cut in half

In a medium bowl combine first 8 ingredients, blend well. Spoon into a second smaller bowl that is just large enough to hold mixture. Cover and refrigerate 8 hours or longer (overnight if you wish). When ready to assemble and serve salad, turn out dressing onto a large platter; sprinkle surface with caviar, and surround with lettuce wedges and halves of cold hard-cooked eggs.

• *Makes 8 servings.*

NOTES: Caviar makes this seemingly simple salad one of the most impressive, as well as delicious, that you can serve. Fresh caviar would of course be superb, but a top-brand salted, pressed caviar will also do nicely.

The quality of the dressing also depends on the quality of the remaining ingredients. Homemade mayonnaise *(see p. 57)* is a positive must, as are top-quality catsup and vinegar, real Tabasco sauce, and the best brand of Worcestershire (this last is wrapped in brown paper; you can't miss it). The quality of the salad, however, no matter how perfect the dressing, will also depend on the lettuce. Crisp Boston lettuce is my choice—although it is not as firm as iceberg lettuce, it has much more flavor. Choose very fresh heads, and they will cut nicely into compact wedges.

MENU
SUGGESTION

Salade à la Russe
Crusty Hard Rolls
(heated and buttered)
Chilled Dry White Wine
Pineapple-Raspberry Sorbet
Cream Cheese Loaf Cake (see p. 144)

California Cottage Cheese Salad

4 cups cottage cheese
1 medium-size tart apple, peeled, cored, and diced
2 or 3 stalks celery, diced
1 medium cucumber, peeled, seeded, and diced
1 medium tomato, seeded and diced
¼ cup minced chives or tops of green onion
½ cup sour cream
Salt
Pepper
Paprika
Poppy-seed dressing *(see p. 59)*

Mix first 7 ingredients, season to taste. Refrigerate until ready to serve. *(See Menu Suggestion on p. 54.)*

NOTE: Serve on lettuce leaves, in scooped-out tomato shells, or in fresh peach halves or avocado halves. Spoon poppy seed dressing over each serving.

NOTE: Serve as a dip with unsalted wheat crackers.

AND MORE NOTES: To seed tomatoes, cut firm but ripe tomatoes in half, gently squeeze out seeds and pulp. Sprinkle with a little salt. Turn upside down on paper toweling to drain; cut on chopping board into small dice or strips; blot dry with paper toweling. Added to any salad, this dry tomato dice adds tomato flavor but no juice to water down the salad.

MENU
SUGGESTION

California Cottage Cheese Salad
Poppy Seed Dressing
Hard Crusty Rolls
(split, toasted, and spread with anchovy butter)
Strawberry Sorbet
with Fresh or Frozen Blueberries
French Gaufrettes
Coffee

Spinach Salad with Avocado, Orange, and Bacon

4 Tbs. lemon juice
6 Tbs. mild salad oil
1 tsp. sugar
Salt
Coarsely ground black pepper
1 lb. fresh spinach, washed, trimmed, all tough leaves
    removed, leaves torn into bite-size pieces
1 medium avocado, peeled, seeded, cut into bite-size cubes
1 or 2 navel oranges, peeled and sliced, slices
    cut into quarters
8 slices crisp cooked bacon, crumbled

Combine lemon juice, oil, sugar, salt, and pepper to taste. Beat until blended and creamy. Pour over spinach, avocado, orange, and bacon. Toss and serve.

• *Makes 4 servings.*

MENU
SUGGESTION

Spinach Salad
with
Avocado, Orange, and Bacon
Ripe Brie or Camembert
Lightly Toasted French Bread
Ripe Pears   Walnuts
Dry White Wine

SALAD DRESSINGS

Oil and Vinegar Dressing for Green Salads

(Variously known as vinaigrette, or "French" dressing)

Most so-called "gourmet" recipes call for olive oil, but the best oil for salad dressing is not olive oil, at least not in this country. In Italy or France, where truly fresh olive oil is available, it is ideal. But, for the most part, the olive oil available in the United States is not. For a very simple reason: it is almost invariably rancid. Fresh olive oil is pale green in color and has a faintly sweet, nutty taste. The deep golden tint of most bottled or canned olive oil is proof of its rancidity. Not only is it bad-tasting, it's actually bad for you. In fact, I really believe rancid olive-oil dressing in the reason many people don't like green salad. The best available oil for salads is pure peanut oil, packed without preservatives or additives; however, peanut oil can go rancid too, so look before you buy. It should appear almost colorless. If it is deep golden in color put it back on the shelf, since it is rancid. Next to peanut oil I like pure safflower oil, available in health-food shops. Since they sell a lot of it you have a good chance of buying truly fresh oil.

In the recipe to follow, a teaspoon of sugar has been added to compensate for the lack of natural sweetness found in fresh olive oil. No, it doesn't taste "sweet," it just tastes very good. Try it on someone who "just doesn't like green salads"; you'll be amazed.

1 tsp. sugar
1 Tbs. white wine vinegar
Pinch of salt
½ tsp. freshly ground black pepper
½ cup peanut or safflower oil

Dissolve the sugar in the vinegar; add salt, pepper, and oil. Beat well with a fork until slightly thick. If made ahead of time beat again just before serving.

• *Makes enough dressing for 4 servings of salad. A salad should be dressed, not drowned.*

Greenery Salad Dressing

Made in minutes in your processor or blender, this is an especially good dressing for a summer salad of cold cooked lima beans, beets, and corn.

2 Tbs. chopped chives
½ cup chopped parsley
½ cup chopped watercress
8 shallots, peeled
2 tsp. Dijon mustard
1 tsp. grated horseradish
2 egg yolks
⅓ cup lemon juice
1 cup salad oil

Combine all ingredients in processor or blender. Process until smooth. Transfer to small bowl, cover, and refrigerate until ready to use.

• *Makes about 2½ cups.*

Mayonnaise

Homemade mayonnaise is a snap to make with an electric hand mixer. It can be made in a blender or processor, but it will not be as thick as when beaten with the rotary action of a mixer.

2 egg yolks
2 Tbs. vinegar or lemon juice
1/2 tsp. sugar
1 tsp. Dijon mustard
1–2 dashes Tabasco sauce
Salt (about 1/4 tsp.)
1 cup mild salad oil (*not* olive oil)

In a small bowl combine all ingredients except oil, beat with rotary beater at high speed until frothy. Add oil a small amount at a time. Beat until each addition of oil is thoroughly incorporated. After final addition, beat an extra minute or two to assure thickness. Cover and refrigerate until ready to use.

• *Makes about 1 1/2 cups.*

Green Mayonnaise

A lovely dressing for aspic salads or fresh cooked and chilled shrimp or crabmeat.

1 cup shredded raw spinach
1/2 cup chopped parsley
1/2 cup chopped chives
3 Tbs. capers
1/4 tsp. Java pepper
1 1/2 cups homemade mayonnaise (*see above*)

Combine all ingredients except mayonnaise in work bowl of food processor. Process until almost liquid.* Combine with

*Vegetables may be chopped by hand, using a sharp cleaver and a wooden chopping board. Chop very fine, until almost pulverized.

mayonnaise in a small bowl, blend with a fork. Cover and refrigerate until ready to serve.
* *Makes about 2½ cups.*

Caviar Salad Dressing

This is so elegant you can serve it with just plain hearts of Bibb or Boston lettuce and have something pretty special. It's also super good for cold seafood; or serve over cold, sliced hard-cooked eggs as a first course or luncheon entrée.

>   1 cup sour cream
>   1 cup homemade mayonnaise *(see p. 57)*
>   2 Tbs. grated horseradish
>   1 (3½-oz.) jar red caviar

Combine all ingredients in a small bowl, blend well with a fork. Cover and refrigerate until ready to use.

Mustard Mayonnaise

This mayonnaise requires much less oil than regular mayonnaise. It is not as thick, but is less calorie-laden than the classic recipe.

>   1 hard-cooked egg yolk
>   1 egg yolk
>   2 tsp. Dijon (or similar) mustard
>   2 tsp. lemon juice
>   6 Tbs. peanut or safflower oil
>   Salt
>   Coarsely ground black pepper

Put the hard-cooked egg yolk in a small bowl and mash until smooth; add raw egg yolk and beat until blended. Beat in the lemon juice, then slowly add the oil, beating as added. Season to taste with salt and pepper.
* *Makes about ½ cup.*

Poppy-Seed Dressing

This is a classic salad dressing for fruit, and equally delicious on Bibb lettuce. A real chore to make before the advent of the processor, it now takes only minutes and no effort at all. (It may also be made in a blender, but in this case the onion should be grated before adding. Use the fine side of the grater only.)

1 tsp. mustard
1 tsp. salt
½ cup vinegar
½ small onion, peeled
1 cup sugar
1½ cups salad oil (*not* olive oil)
2 Tbs. poppy seeds

Combine mustard, salt, vinegar, onion, and sugar in work bowl of processor. Process briefly to blend; with the motor running, gradually add oil. Add poppy seeds, process a final second or two.

• *Makes 2½ cups dressing.*

ANTIPASTOS

Vegetable Antipasto

½ small cauliflower, broken into small flowerets
2 or 3 stalks broccoli, tops broken into flowerets, stalks
     trimmed, then cut lengthwise into matchstick strips
2 carrots, scraped and cut lengthwise into matchstick strips
2 stalks celery, cut into 1-inch pieces
¼ lb. fresh green beans, trimmed
1 small jar pitted black olives, drained
1 jar big English pickled onions, drained
1 cup water
1 cup wine vinegar
½ cup salad oil
2 Tbs. sugar
1 tsp. dry mustard
1 clove garlic, peeled, crushed
1 tsp. oregano
1 tsp. salt
Coarsely ground black pepper

In a large enamelized or stainless steel pot combine all ingredients; bring to a boil, lower heat; let simmer 10 minutes.
Cool in cooking liquid, refrigerate in a covered glass or ceramic
storage dish 6 to 8 hours or 1 to 2 days. Drain and serve on
lettuce leaves.
• *Makes 6 servings.*

MENU
SUGGESTION

Vegetable Antipasto
Sliced Italian Salami
Italian Bread
Prune Whip, Italian Style (see p. 156)
Coffee

Antipasto Supper

    1 cup salad oil
    ¼ cup red wine vinegar
    2 tsp. salt
    1 tsp. mixed Italian herbs
    1 tsp. sugar
    Coarsely ground black pepper
    2 or 3 cups cooked red kidney beans
        (canned or home cooked)
    1 or 2 cups cooked white navy beans
        (canned or home cooked)
    1 cup thinly sliced celery
    1 head Boston lettuce, washed, dried, shredded
    2 large tomatoes, cored, cut into wedges
    ½ lb. provolone cheese, thinly sliced and rolled
    ½ lb. Genoa salami, thinly sliced and rolled
    1 (2-oz.) can rolled anchovies with capers, drained
    Italian (packed in oil) ripe olives

Combine oil, vinegar, salt, herbs, sugar, and a goodly amount of
black pepper in container of electric blender or food processor.
Blend or process until well mixed. Combine beans and celery
in a bowl, add about ½ cup dressing, toss to blend. Cover, chill.
To serve, line a large platter with lettuce leaves. Mound beans
and celery in center. Arrange tomato wedges, cheese, and salami
around bean mixture. Top bean mixture with anchovies, garnish
platter with ripe olives. Serve remaining dressing separately.

NOTE: This is a supper of hors d'oeuvres. Serve with crisp, hot
garlic bread and red wine. For dessert add espresso and Italian
Amaretti cookies.

Grilled Meals

GRILLING was the primitive hunter's only means of cooking his meat, and ever since, people have loved the taste, flavor, and aroma of grilled foods. Whether the result is a hamburger grilled in the back yard or the most lavish mixed grill ever served in the hallowed dining room of the most exclusive London club, grilling was, is, and always will be the most delicious way to cook foods. So what else is new? There is indeed nothing new about grilled meat or seafood. What is new is the sudden popularity of grilled *meals:* not simply meat alone, but grilled vegetables and potatoes as well; and they taste fabulous. Just wait until you taste grilled sweet potatoes, grilled onions, zucchini, tomatoes, eggplant, and Idaho potatoes—they are simply great. It's all part of a new concept of our new cook-it-all-at-once cuisine; of easy, effortless, yet super-good meals. It's also part of our new consciousness about calories, high cholesterol, and excess fat; in short, it's a "now" way to plan, cook, and serve imaginative, great-tasting food.

Grilling can be done on the new high-heat indoor grills, on the top-surface grills of the new wonder stoves, outdoors on a deluxe gas grill, or just over a plain old charcoal grill set up wherever it's handy, on a terrace or in the back yard. The place is not important; what is important is that grilling does require super-high heat to seal the surface of the food. That way meats are crusty brown on the outside, juicy and tender within; vegetables done to a turn but still retaining their fresh flavor; and everything delicious.

Aside from the just plain wonderful taste, grilled foods are undoubtedly good for you as well. The dieter has long known that the high-powered, great-tasting way to lose weight was to stick to grilled meats or fish. But there's more to the grill nutrition story than just calorie count: grilled foods are lower in cholesterol and higher in vitamin and mineral content than those cooked by almost any other method. Vegetables especially retain all their "good for you" qualities when grilled.

In short, grilled meals are indeed part of our new thinking about food, part of the "kitchen revolution" which has produced meals that are better tasting and better for you with ease, speed, and convenience.

The Major's Steak-and-Mushroom Grill

1 (12-oz.) can beer
½ cup chili sauce
¼ cup vegetable oil
1 Tbs. Dijon mustard
1 tsp. Worcestershire sauce
1 clove garlic, peeled, crushed
1 (3- to 3½-lb.) sirloin steak, about 1½ to 2 inches thick
4 Tbs. butter
1 Tbs. more vegetable oil
12 to 16 large mushroom caps
Coarsely ground black pepper
3 medium tomatoes, cut in half
Salt

Combine first 6 ingredients in a saucepan; simmer 30 minutes. Remove and discard garlic. Cool. Place steak in shallow nonmetal dish, pour marinade over steak. Allow to stand 1 to 2 hours at room temperature. Drain steak, reserve marinade.

In a small skillet melt butter with oil; place near grill.

Brush steak with marinade and sprinkle with pepper. Place on grill about 4 inches from hot coals (about 3 inches over gas or electric heat). Over coals, grill 8 to 10 minutes, turn, brush with marinade, grill a final 8 to 10 minutes or until cooked to desired degree of rareness. If using gas or electric grill follow manufacturer's chart for timing. Either way, don't cook this fine steak more than medium rare.

Dip mushroom caps in butter and place on grill about 10 minutes before steak is done. Dip cut halves of tomatoes in butter and place cut side down on grill; grill 5 minutes. Turn, baste with butter, and continue to grill until soft but not falling apart. Sprinkle with salt just before removing from grill.

• *Makes 6 servings.*

TIPS FOR BUILDING A CHARCOAL FIRE: If using outdoor charcoal grill, start fire about 30 to 45 minutes before grilling meat. To ensure that charcoal burns evenly in allotted time, measure by covering bottom of grill or coal rack with a single layer of charcoal; then rearrange charcoal in a pyramid stack in the center of grill. Prepare with charcoal lighter fluid and light. When coals are ash gray and hot with no flame, respread to cover grill in a single layer. If using gas or electric grill follow manufacturer's direction for preheating.

Grilled Steak with Potatoes, Zucchini, and Onions

If this is to be an outdoor cookout why not serve the best of summer desserts—cold watermelon?

½ cup vegetable oil
1 (8-oz.) can tomato sauce
1 Tbs. red wine vinegar
1 tsp. Worcestershire sauce
1 tsp. sugar
½ tsp. salt
1 clove garlic, peeled, crushed
2 (6- to 8-oz.) cube steaks
¼ lb. butter
2 Tbs. vegetable oil
1 large oval baking potato, scrubbed, cut lengthwise
   into thin slices
2 medium zucchini, trimmed, cut lengthwise into slices
2 small white onions, cut in half horizontally (*not* peeled)
Salt

Combine first 7 ingredients in a shallow baking dish; mix well. Add meat, turn to coat with marinade. Let stand at room temperature 1 to 2 hours, turning meat in marinade several times.

If using an outdoor charcoal grill, follow directions for preparing charcoal on page 64. If using electric or gas grill, preheat according to manufacturer's instructions.

In a small skillet melt butter with oil; place near grill.

Dip potato and zucchini slices and cut side of onion halves in melted butter mixture. Arrange on grill. Grill vegetables, turning and basting frequently with butter-oil mixture, until tender through center and lightly browned—about 15 minutes. Sprinkle vegetables with salt just before removing from grill.

When vegetables have cooked 5 to 10 minutes place meat on grill, pour marinade into a small skillet, remove and discard garlic. Set aside. When using outdoor charcoal grill, grill steaks 2 minutes on each side (turning once) for rare, 3 minutes on each side (turning once) for medium rare, and 4 minutes on each side (turning once) for medium well. If using gas or electric grill follow manufacturer's chart for degree of doneness desired. Heat marinade and serve as sauce.

• *Makes 2 servings.*

Grilled Steak and Potato Kabobs

This is a delicious meal in one; a light red wine such as a Beaujolais would be perfect. Flaming cherry tart would make a gorgeous ending.

2 green peppers, seeded, cut into 1-inch squares
16 very small new potatoes
8 slices bacon, cut in half
3 lbs. top round steak, cut into 1½-inch cubes
Meat tenderizer
24 large mushroom caps
1 cup dry red wine
1 clove garlic, peeled, crushed
24 cherry tomatoes

Parboil green-pepper squares in water to cover for 5 minutes; drain and blot dry. Steam or boil new potatoes until sufficiently tender to pierce easily with a small kitchen knife. Place bacon in a heavy skillet over low heat until partially cooked but not crisp; drain. Sprinkle meat with tenderizer and let stand at room temperature for 30 minutes; sprinkle again with tenderizer. Put meat, mushrooms, and wine in a shallow glass baking dish, add garlic. Cover and let stand at room temperature 1 to 2 hours. Drain.

If using an outdoor charcoal grill, follow directions for preparing charcoal on page 64. If using electric or gas grill, follow manufacturer's directions for preheating.

Wrap a half slice of partially cooked bacon around each cooked potato.

Thread meat cubes, bacon-wrapped potatoes, mushrooms, cherry tomatoes, and green-pepper squares alternately on skewers. Grill, turning skewers often, 10 to 15 minutes on charcoal grill, or until desired degree of doneness. If using gas or electric grill, follow manufacturer's chart or grill until done to taste.

• *Makes 6 servings.*

Lamb Chop Mixed Grill

Good enough to deserve a really good wine: a Bordeaux such as Château Calon-Ségur would be perfect. Of course, with a wine this good, a great cheese is the very best dessert to accompany the last drop of wine in style.

8 little link pork sausages
8 chicken livers
2 Tbs. butter
1 Tbs. soy sauce
1 Tbs. sugar
Salt
4 slices bacon, each cut in half
8 large mushroom caps (reserve stems for another use)
4 rib lamb chops, each about 1 inch thick

1 clove garlic, peeled, split
2 more Tbs. butter, softened
Salt
Pepper
4 slices (canned) pineapple
2 more Tbs. butter, softened

With a small sharp knife prick each sausage link in several places; put in a small skillet and cover with water. Let simmer 10 minutes over medium heat, drain, set aside.

Use kitchen shears to trim off and discard all white connective tissue from chicken livers. Melt the 2 Tbs. butter in a small skillet; add chicken livers and sauté only until firm. Sprinkle with soy sauce, sugar, and salt. Wrap each liver in a half slice of bacon, set aside.

Wipe mushrooms clean with a damp cloth. Rub each lamb chop with a split garlic clove; spread with about 2 Tbs. of the soft butter.

If using outdoor charcoal grill, follow directions for preparing charcoal on page 64. If using electric or gas grill, preheat, following manufacturer's instructions.

Place chops, bacon-wrapped chicken livers, and sausage links on grill, 5 or 6 inches from hot coals; or 3 to 4 inches over electric or gas grill. Grill chops 6 to 7 minutes for rare, 9 to 10 minutes for medium-well done. If using gas or electric grill, follow manufacturer's chart for desired degree of doneness. Turn chops once or twice on the grill. About 5 minutes before meat is done, grill bacon-wrapped chicken livers and sausage, turning them often until bacon is crisp, sausage crusty and well-browned. Brush mushroom caps and pineapple slices with remaining soft butter. Add to grill about 3 minutes before meats are cooked. Grill, turning once or twice, until mushrooms are tender, pineapple slices hot and flecked with brown.

• *Makes 4 servings.*

Grilled Pork Chops with Sweet Potatoes, Green Peppers, and Pineapple

¼ cup vegetable oil
Juice from 1 (8-oz.) can sliced unsweetened pineapple
Juice from 1 large lemon
2 Tbs. cider vinegar
2 cloves garlic, peeled, crushed
4 loin pork chops, about 1 inch thick
2 medium green peppers
1 large oval sweet potato, scrubbed and cut lengthwise into
    thin oval slices
4 slices (canned) pineapple in natural unsweetened juice

Combine first 5 ingredients in a shallow baking dish; mix well. Add chops, turn to coat with marinade. Cover and marinate several hours at room temperature or overnight in refrigerator.

If using outdoor charcoal grill, follow directions for preparing charcoal on page 64. If using electric or gas grill, preheat following manufacturer's instructions.

Remove chops from marinade, place 4 to 5 inches above heat, reserve marinade. Place green peppers on grill, laying them on one side. After 4 to 5 minutes check the peppers. When the skin toward the fire is charred, turn another side of the peppers toward the fire. Continue to turn every 3 to 4 minutes until the peppers are charred on all sides. Remove and set aside until sufficiently cool to handle. Use a small knife to scrape off the charred skin, discard the seeds. Cut the peppers into strips. Either return the strips to edge of the grill where they will stay warm or set them aside until the chops and potatoes are cooked, then reheat briefly.

Grill the chops 20 to 30 minutes or until no longer pink in center on outdoor charcoal grill, 4 to 5 inches from heat. When using an electric or gas grill follow manufacturer's chart for degree of doneness desired. About 15 minutes before chops are cooked, add potato slices to the grill and baste with reserved marinade. Baste chops with marinade also. Turn and baste chops and potatoes several times during the last few minutes of grilling. Add the pineapple slices and return the green-pepper strips to the grill about 5 minutes before the meat and potatoes are ready to serve. They need only be heated.

• *Makes 4 servings.*

SOUTHERN-STYLE-SUPPER
SUGGESTION

Mint Juleps
Grilled Pork Chops with
Sweet Potatoes, Green Peppers, and Pineapple
Popovers
Burnt Sugar Ice Cream (see p. 164)

Grilled Ham with Champagne Sauce, Eggplant, and Apples

Make this extra special by serving homemade rolls and finishing off with champagne!

> 1 slice (1-inch thick) precooked ham, about 1½ lbs.
> ½ cup champagne (or substitute ginger ale)
> ½ cup orange juice
> ¼ cup firmly packed brown sugar
> 2 Tbs. vegetable oil
> 1 tsp. dry mustard
> ¼ tsp. ground ginger
> 1 small eggplant
> 2 small tart apples
> 4 Tbs. butter
> 1 more Tbs. vegetable oil
> Salt

Score fat edge of ham. Combine next 6 ingredients; pour over ham in a shallow baking dish. Let stand at room temperature 1 to 2 hours, spooning marinade over ham several times.

If using outdoor charcoal grill, follow directions for preparing charcoal on page 64. If using an electric or gas grill, preheat according to manufacturer's instructions.

Cut eggplant in half, sprinkle cut side with salt. Place in a colander, cut side against colander sides; let stand about 15 minutes to drain. Rinse with clear water, blot dry. Cut each apple into 2 thick slices, discarding end pieces.

In a small skillet melt butter with oil; place near grill.

Drain and place ham slice on grill, reserve marinade. Grill 15 minutes, brushing with marinade several times. Turn and brush with marinade. Dip apple slices and cut side of eggplant in butter mixture, arrange on grill. Grill 10 to 15 minutes or until fork-tender but not browned, turning several times and basting with butter. Sprinkle with salt. Grill ham steak a total of 25 to 30 minutes over charcoal fire. If using gas or electric grill, follow manufacturer's chart for timing.

Heat remaining marinade and serve with ham.

• *Makes 4 servings.*

Chicken Mixed Grill, Italian Style

Nice to serve, if this is a summer cookout, with spritzers— half wine and half club soda, poured over lots of crushed ice.

> 1 (8-oz.) can Italian-style tomato sauce
> ½ cup vegetable oil
> ½ cup orange juice
> ¼ cup red wine vinegar
> 1 tsp. mixed Italian herbs
> 1 tsp. salt
> ½ tsp. pepper
> 1 clove garlic, peeled, minced
> 1 (2½ to 3-lb.) broiler-fryer, quartered
> 4 Tbs. butter
> 1 Tbs. vegetable oil
> 2 very small eggplants
> 1 small zucchini
> 2 medium tomatoes, each cut in half
> Salt

Combine first 8 ingredients, blend well; pour over chicken in a shallow baking dish. Let stand at room temperature 4 to 6 hours, turning occasionally.

If using outdoor charcoal grill, follow directions for preparing charcoal on page 64. Preheat gas or electric grill, following manufacturer's instructions.

Cut each eggplant in half, sprinkle cut sides with salt; place in colander, cut side against sides of colander. Let drain about 15 minutes. Rinse with cold water, blot dry. Trim and cut zucchini lengthwise into thin slices.

Melt butter with oil in a small skillet; place near grill.

Remove chicken from marinade and place bone side down on grill. Grill 45 minutes to 1 hour over hot coals or until tender, or grill on electric or gas grill, following manufacturer's chart, until tender; turn chicken and brush with marinade about every 15 minutes.

Certain meats with high fat content, as well as chicken skin, will cause flame flare-ups on an outdoor charcoal grill. If this occurs, coals may be cooled by spraying with a light spray of water or allowing more coal-preparation time.

About 15 minutes before chicken is cooked, dip cut side of eggplants and tomatoes in melted butter mixture and place on grill, cut side down. Dip zucchini strips in butter and arrange on grill. Grill eggplants and tomatoes about 5 minutes. Turn cut side up, brush with butter, and continue to grill until soft but not browned, turning cut side down for last minute of cooking. Grill the zucchini for about the same length of time, dipping the strips in butter and turning them several times. They are done when soft and flecked with brown. Sprinkle vegetables with salt just before removing from grill. Cut each eggplant half into 2 servings.

* *Makes 4 servings.*

Stir-Fry Meals

THE COOKING METHOD of ancient China is the newest thing going in today's kitchens. And for good reasons. First, it produces a complete and completely delicious meal in minutes; second, it's very much in tune with today's lighter, more interesting meals. The combinations of foods that can be successfully stir-fried are almost limitless, and the method adapts with equal ease to meat, chicken, or seafood. Everything tastes great: meats are juicy and flavorful, and vegetables tender-crisp; the whole thing is so simple that stir-fry-at-the-table parties have become the new way to entertain.

A wok is essential for stir-frying. Unchanged in design for thousands of years, the wok's shallow bowl shape allows foods to cook quickly in a very small amount of oil. Ingredients are sliced paper-thin, cut into matchlike strips, or finely shredded; they are then literally stir-fried in the hot oil for a few moments. A small amount of liquid is added, and the wok covered to allow a brief steaming time. Leafy greenery such as spinach or Chinese cabbage is added at the last moment, and that's it— dinner is served.

Stir-fry is easy, fast, and actually fun: the only trick is to have all your ingredients ready before you begin to cook. It's such a fast process that there's no time to stop and look for even one forgotten seasoning. So check your recipe before you start.

One word of caution: never substitute solid shortening for oil in stir-frying. Only oil will heat to a sufficiently high temperature without burning or smoking heavily. Olive oil is not recommended, for the same reasons. Use a mild salad oil (peanut oil is best).

If stir-frying is new to you and you are going to add a wok to your "batterie de cuisine," make sure you purchase one heavy enough to do the job. Steel is probably the best choice, and I prefer a wok that is used directly on the stove rather than the electric variety. Somehow the electric ones don't seem to get hot enough to suit me. Clean and season your new wok according to the manufacturer's directions; wash it carefully in a mild detergent after each use, and dry really thoroughly. Placing it over low heat for a few moments assures absolute dryness, a must if you are going to prevent rusting. Store your wok in the open if at all possible. Since it is seasoned with oil, it may develop a musty smell if left too long in a closed place. I keep mine right on my kitchen counter. It's a good-looking implement and adds to the decor of any kitchen.

Stir-Fried Beef with Tomatoes and Peas

> 1 (10-oz.) package frozen peas
> 1 lb. fillet of beef, about 1 inch thick
> 1 Tbs. peanut oil
> 1 large mild onion, peeled, chopped
> 2 or 3 firm but ripe tomatoes, cut into wedges
> 1 tsp. sugar
> Soy sauce (about 2 Tbs.)
> 4 Tbs. chicken stock or water
> 1 tsp. cornstarch
> 4 more Tbs. chicken stock or water
> 2–3 drops sesame oil *(optional)*
> 3 to 4 cups hot cooked rice

Place frozen peas in a colander, hold under hot running tap water until thawed, gently lifting and stirring with your hands until peas feel warm; set aside.

Cut meat across the grain into thin strips (this is done easily if the meat is placed in the freezer until very cold and firm but not frozen).

Heat the oil in a wok; add onion and stir-fry about 30 seconds. Push the onion to the sides of the wok, add beef strips, stir-fry until no longer pink. Add tomato wedges and peas. Stir-fry 30 seconds. Sprinkle with sugar and soy sauce; pour in the 4 Tbs. of stock, cover and steam 30 seconds. Stir cornstarch into additional 4 Tbs. stock, add sesame oil; blend and pour into wok. Stir mixture over medium heat until liquid thickens. Serve over rice.

• *Makes 4 servings.*

★

Stir-Fried Beef and Cabbage

> 1 lb. top round of beef in one piece, about 1 inch thick
> 1 Tbs. finely shredded ginger root
> 1 tsp. sugar
> 1 Tbs. peanut oil
> 2 Tbs. soy sauce
> 2 more Tbs. peanut oil
> 2–3 drops sesame oil *(optional)*
> 2 cups finely shredded cabbage, packed down
>   (about ½ small head cabbage)
> 4 stalks celery, very thinly sliced, "slanty-eyed"
>   (on the diagonal)
> 1 small carrot, scraped and finely shredded
> ¼ cup stock or water
> 2 tsp. cornstarch
> 2 Tbs. stock or water
> 2 Tbs. dry sherry
> 3–4 cups hot cooked rice
> Additional soy sauce (about 2 Tbs.)

Cut beef across the grain into very thin slices (you can do this easily if you place the meat in the freezer until very cold and firm but not frozen). Combine shredded ginger, sugar, the 1 Tbs. oil, and 2 Tbs. soy sauce; rub mixture into meat slices, let stand at room temperature 30 minutes.

Heat remaining 2 Tbs. oil in a wok. Add the meat slices and stir-fry until no longer pink. Add cabbage, celery, and carrot. Stir-fry 30 seconds. Pour in the ¼ cup stock, cover, and steam 2 to 3 minutes, or until cabbage has lost its raw taste but is still crisp. Stir cornstarch into remaining 2 Tbs. stock, add sherry. Stir into vegetable and meat mixture. Stir-fry a final 30 seconds. Serve over rice. Add soy sauce to taste.

• *Makes 4 servings.*

Stir-Fried Beef with Mushrooms and Celery

This stir-fry dish is really a complete meal. Add a dessert and after-dinner coffee, and it's all any epicure could ask for.

> 1 (8-oz.) package very fine noodles
> 1 Tbs. peanut or safflower oil
> 1/2 lb. tender lean beef
> 1 Tbs. cornstarch
> 1 Tbs. soy sauce
> 1 (8-oz.) package mushrooms
> 4 to 6 stalks celery
> 3 Tbs. more peanut or safflower oil
> 1/4 cup water
> Soy sauce

Cook noodles in a large pot of lightly salted water until barely tender. Drain into a bowl, add the 1 Tbs. oil, toss briefly. Set aside.

Cut meat into thin, narrow strips; place in a bowl. Stir cornstarch into soy sauce; pour over beef strips, stir to blend. Trim stem ends from mushrooms, cut across into thin T-shaped slices. Thinly slice celery on the diagonal.

Heat oil in wok, add beef strips; stir-fry until no longer pink; remove from wok, set aside. Add mushrooms and celery to wok. Stir-fry 30 seconds. Add water. Cover wok and let vegetables steam 3 to 4 minutes, stirring occasionally. Return beef to wok. Stir-fry until meat is hot, vegetables barely tender. Stir in noodles. Serve at once with additional soy sauce if desired.

Stir-Fried Ham with Green Cabbage

1 large head green cabbage, cored and shredded
Cold water
2 Tbs. sugar
2 Tbs. salt
¼ cup butter
1 to 2 cups chopped leftover baked ham
¼ cup water
Pepper

In a large bowl cover cabbage with cold water, stir in sugar and salt. Refrigerate for several hours. Drain, rinse well. Melt butter in a large, deep skillet, add cabbage and ham. Stir and fry 1 to 2 minutes; add water. Cover and let steam until cabbage is tender and no raw taste remains but it is still slightly crisp. Correct seasoning with pepper.

NOTE: Add steamed new potatoes, and dinner is served.

MORE NOTES: No ham? Cook the cabbage as directed, add crisp, cooked crumbled bacon, or leave out bacon and serve the cabbage with any leftover sliced cold meat.

Stir-Fried Chicken with Lemon Sauce, Shredded Lettuce, and Almonds

2 tsp. cornstarch
2 tsp. water
2 Tbs. lemon juice
½ cup chicken stock
1 tsp. finely grated lemon peel
1 Tbs. peanut oil
1 clove garlic, peeled, crushed flat
1 cube (1 inch) ginger root, crushed flat
2 whole chicken breasts, skinned, boned,
    cut into bite-size pieces

2 cups (packed down) shredded lettuce
½ cup slivered toasted almonds
Hot cooked rice

Stir cornstarch into water; add lemon juice, stock, and grated lemon peel. Blend, set aside. Heat wok; add oil, garlic, and ginger root. Stir and fry until garlic begins to brown; remove and discard garlic and ginger root. Add chicken pieces. Stir-fry until white and firm, about 1 minute. Stir cornstarch and stock mixture to reblend, pour over chicken; stir until liquid thickens. Stir in lettuce only enough to blend with chicken and sauce. Serve at once over hot cooked rice. Sprinkle with toasted slivered almonds.

   • *Makes about 4 servings.*

Stir-Fried Duck with Scallions

1 (3½- to 4-lb.) duck, roasted and cooled *(see p. 78)*
2 Tbs. finely shredded ginger root
1 tsp. salt
1 Tbs. vegetable oil
2 tsp. cornstarch
4 Tbs. chicken stock or broth
2 Tbs. dry sherry
1 tsp. sugar
3 Tbs. soy sauce
2 more Tbs. oil
4 scallions or green onions, chopped
1 cup cooked green beans
3 to 4 cups cooked rice
4 oz. slivered almonds

Cut meat from duck into bite-size pieces, including some of the crisp skin. Combine shredded ginger root with salt, add the 1 Tbs. oil; rub mixture into duck pieces. Let stand at room temperature 30 minutes.

   Combine cornstarch, stock, sherry, sugar, and soy sauce; blend, set aside.

Heat the 2 Tbs. oil in wok, add green onions, stir-fry 30 seconds. Add the duck, stir-fry about 1 minute. Restir the cornstarch mixture, add to wok, and stir-fry 30 seconds. Stir in peas and almonds. Stir until heated and sauce has thickened. Serve over rice.

• *Makes 4 servings.*

To roast duck:
    1 (3½- to 4-lb.) duck (thawed, if frozen)
    Salt

Preheat oven to 450° F.

Wash the duck, remove and discard excess fat from the body and neck cavities. Rub inside and out with salt. Place, breast side up, on rack over shallow roasting pan. Roast 15 minutes. Reduce oven temperature to 350° F. Turn duck on its side, roast 30 minutes. Remove most of the fat from the pan as it accumulates. Turn duck to other side, roast 15 minutes, then turn breast side up and roast for a final 15 minutes or until done. To test, prick thigh meat. When the juices run pale yellow, duck is done. Let duck cool to room temperature.

Stir-Fried Chicken Livers with Shrimp and Broccoli

    1 bunch broccoli (about 1 lb.)
    ½ lb. chicken livers
    ½ lb. shrimp, shelled and deveined
    ¼ cup soy sauce
    2 Tbs. oil
    1 1-inch cube ginger root, peeled, finely minced
    1 tsp. sugar
    3 Tbs. chicken stock or broth (or water)
    2 Tbs. dry sherry
    3 to 4 cups hot cooked rice

Wash and trim broccoli, remove and discard outer leaves, cut off tops, and break into small flowerets. Cut stalks into 1-inch matchstick strips. Soak flowerets and strips in salted water 10 to 15 minutes, drain. Rinse with clear water. Cut each chicken liver in half, remove all white connective tissue; combine with shrimp in a nonmetal bowl. Add ¼ cup soy sauce. Let stand 15 to 20 minutes, drain, reserve soy sauce.

Heat oil in wok. Add broccoli strips, stir-fry about 1 minute. Add chicken livers and shrimp; stir-fry about 1 minute or until chicken livers are firm. Sprinkle with sugar. Add broccoli flowerets, stock or broth (or water), and sherry. Stir-fry 30 seconds. Add reserved soy sauce. Cover and steam about 1 minute. Stir-fry a final 30 seconds or until almost all liquid has evaporated. Serve over rice.

• *Makes 4 servings.*

Stir-Fried Shrimp and Pork

Make the sauce first: this is a 2-minute stir-fry.

2 Tbs. peanut oil
1–2 drops sesame oil
1 lb. large shrimp, peeled, deveined
Lean cooked pork, cut into thin strips
    (about 1 cup packed down)
¼ cup thinly sliced green onion
Chow sauce (see p. 80)
3–4 cups hot cooked rice

Chow sauce

1 lightly beaten egg
2 Tbs. (bottled) Chinese plum sauce
2 Tbs. soy sauce
1 tsp. sugar
1 tsp. cornstarch
2 Tbs. water

Heat oils in wok, add shrimp, pork strips, and scallions; stir-fry until shrimp turn pink. Add Chow Sauce, stir until sauce is bubbly hot and has thickened. Serve over rice.

• *Makes 4 servings.*

To prepare Chow Sauce:

Combine egg, plum sauce, soy sauce, and sugar; blend well. Stir cornstarch into water to make a paste. Stir into egg mixture and reblend just before using.

Sweet-and-Sour Stir-Fried Pork

2 or 3 large stalks broccoli
4 to 6 green onions
Leftover roast pork, sufficient to make 1½ to 2 cups
    pork strips
6 to 8 water chestnuts
1 (8-oz.) can pineapple chunks
1 Tbs. vinegar
¼ cup soy sauce
1 Tbs. cornstarch
1 Tbs. peanut or safflower oil
½ tsp. crushed red pepper
1 to 2 Tbs. water
1 cup fresh bean sprouts
2 Tbs. toasted sesame seeds
Cooked noodles

Wash broccoli thoroughly in cold salted water, rinse in clear cold water. Cut stems from tops; break tops into flowerets. Cut stalks across into 1-inch pieces, cut pieces into thin "matchsticks." Cut pork into thin slices, cut slices into ½-inch strips. Coarsely chop water chestnuts. Drain pineapple chunks; combine juice with vinegar and soy sauce, stir in cornstarch and red pepper.

Heat oil in wok. Add broccoli stalks and green onion; stir-fry about 1 minute. Add about 1 Tbs. water, cover and steam about 1 minute. Add broccoli flowerets, pork, water chestnuts, pineapple chunks, and bean sprouts. Stir-fry about 30 seconds, cover, and steam about 30 seconds. Repeat until vegetables are barely tender, adding a little water if mixture becomes dry. Stir pineapple juice–soy sauce mixture to reblend; pour over vegetables and meat. Stir-fry until sauce thickens. Serve over cooked noodles.

• *Makes about 4 servings.*

Stir-Fried Shrimp with Canadian Bacon, Mushrooms, and Cucumber

1 lb. large shrimp, shelled and deveined
1 clove garlic, peeled, crushed
1 1-inch cube ginger root, peeled, minced
2 Tbs. peanut or safflower oil
1 more Tbs. peanut or safflower oil
1 medium-size white onion, peeled, chopped
½ lb. mushrooms, trimmed, cut across into thin T-slices
¼ lb. Canadian bacon, cut into thin strips
2 small cucumbers, trimmed, cut into ½-inch cubes
1 tsp. sugar
Soy sauce, about 1 Tbs.
Dry sherry, about 2 Tbs.
3 to 4 cups hot cooked rice

Place shrimp and garlic in a shallow nonmetal baking dish, sprinkle with ginger. Add 2 Tbs. oil, stir gently to coat shrimp with oil. Let stand at room temperature for 30 minutes, turning shrimp occasionally in oil (or cover and refrigerate for 1 hour, stirring occasionally). Heat the 1 Tbs. oil in a wok (or 10-inch heavy skillet). Add onion, stir-fry 30 seconds, add mushrooms and Canadian bacon strips. Stir-fry 1 minute. Drain and add shrimp and cucumber cubes. Stir-fry 30 seconds. Sprinkle with sugar and soy sauce, stir-fry 1 minute. Stir in sherry and cook a few seconds longer. Serve on rice.

• *Makes 4 servings.*

Vegetable Sukiyaki

3 Tbs. soy sauce
½ cup chicken stock or broth (or substitute water)
¼ tsp. sugar
1 Tbs. peanut oil
1 drop sesame oil *(optional)*
6 or 8 mushrooms, trimmed, thinly sliced
½ cup chopped green onion
2 cups finely shredded bok choy (or escarole)
2 stalks celery, cut diagonally into thin slices
¼ cup sliced water chestnuts
½ cup bean sprouts
8 oz. tofu (soybean curd), cut into bite-size pieces
Soy sauce
3 to 4 cups hot cooked brown rice

Combine soy sauce, chicken stock or broth, and sugar; set aside.
Heat the oil in a wok, add the mushrooms and onions, stir-fry about 1 minute. Add the bok choy (or escarole), stir-fry 30 seconds. Pour in a little of the soy-sauce mixture. Cover and steam briefly. Add the celery and water chestnuts, plus a little more of the liquid mixture. Cook, alternately stir-frying and steaming, for about 5 minutes, adding liquid as needed. Add the sprouts and tofu, continue to cook only until these ingredients are heated. Add additional soy sauce if desired. Serve over rice.

• *Makes 4 servings.*

Sweet-and-Sour Stir-Fried Vegetables

¼ small head of cabbage (1 wedge), finely shredded
2 or 3 stalks celery, very thinly sliced
6 to 8 large fresh mushrooms, trimmed, sliced
    across into thin T-shapes
Small bunch of broccoli, tops broken into flowerets,
    stalks cut into matchstick strips

½ lb. very young, tender, and fresh green beans or
   1 (10-oz.) package frozen French beans, thawed and
   drained
2 to 2½ Tbs. peanut oil
1 clove garlic, peeled and mashed flat with cleaver
¼ cup water
2 tsp. cornstarch
2 tsp. sugar
2 tsp. white vinegar
½ cup more water
¼ lb. fresh bean sprouts *(optional)*
1 (8-oz.) package thin noodles, cooked

Prepare all vegetables as listed above. Place wok over high heat, add oil and garlic. When oil is hot and garlic begins to brown, remove and discard garlic. Add all vegetables except bean sprouts. Stir-fry 1 minute. Add ¼ cup water, cover and steam 1 to 2 minutes; add bean sprouts, then again stir-fry for 1 minute. Cover and steam 30 seconds.

Stir cornstarch and sugar into vinegar. Add water, stir until blended. Make a well in the center of the vegetables. Pour in cornstarch mixture, stir until it begins to thicken, then stir in the vegetables. Serve very hot over cooked thin noodles.

   • *Makes about 4 servings.*

NOTE: If desired, add about 1 cup (or more if you have it on hand) slivers of leftover roast pork; or add slivered almonds.

Rice

RICE can be at one time delicious, versatile, and easy to cook; or it can be the most tasteless, mushy, and maddening of foods, leaving the frustrated cook with a sticky pot and a dull dinner.

The master recipe which follows promises you that each and every time you prepare rice it will be fluffy, dry, and perfect— the exactly right complement, not only to stir-fried dishes, but to any number of others.

Properly cooked good-quality natural rice is a light, nutritious grain; good and good for you, it is very much in keeping with our new awareness of the need for highly nutritious, lighter food, our continuing revolution against dull, "empty" meals.

THE STIR-FRY COOK'S
METHOD FOR PERFECT RICE

Nothing, absolutely nothing, could be simpler than cooking rice. In fact, it's so easy the only real mystery is how so many pots of gummy, sticky rice have managed to be produced. Oh, well, that is not our concern here; the business at hand is to set down once and for all the super-simple way to cook plain old rice that comes out dry, fluffy, and delicious each and every time. I am not referring to so-called minute or instant rice: I never bothered to waste the extra money these products cost. *Any* rice is quick-cooking and easy. Here's all there is to it. For each cup of raw rice bring about 5 cups of water to a rolling boil, add about 2 teaspoons oil or butter and ¼ teaspoon salt, pour in the rice, and stir. Let come to a boil, turn down the heat to medium, and let simmer until tender. How long depends on the type of rice you are using. Long-grain Carolina rice (the least expensive of all) takes about 15 to 20 minutes; brown rice, my favorite and the most nutritious, about 30. Short-grain Italian rice, superb for flavor but expensive, takes about the same time as brown. Converted rice, about 10 to 15 minutes. When the rice is tender (the only way you can tell is to taste a few grains), dump it all in a colander or sieve and rinse under the hot-water tap. Pour about 2 inches of water in the pot in which the rice was cooked. Bring to just simmering, place the rice, still in the colander, over the hot water, and leave it there until serving time (up to one hour). When you are ready the rice will be too—fluffy, dry, and perfect.

Skilletry

THE NEW ONE-DISH-MEAL CUISINE got its start in *my* kitchen with skilletry; for like just about every other cook in the country, I had a skillet and of course a stove. There was no new equipment to buy—just a new technique to learn, and a fast and easy one at that. Unlike stir-fry, skilletry is not frying at all but sautéing, a time-honored way to cook. It's today's combinations of ingredients that make it news.

It's fast, easy cooking, but what is more to the point, it's truly great eating. Skilletry can be elegant enough for a dinner party or it can be budget-minded, low-cost fare. The principle is the same; only the choice of ingredients varies. Skilletry can come to your rescue when you are too tired to cook, too busy to bother: skillet meals seldom take more than 30 minutes' preparation time, often less. And joy of joys, they are a snap to clean up after. Just one pot for the dishwasher and that's it; a special blessing for the working cook who can't face a kitchen full of dirty dishes no matter how "gourmet" the meal.

Just one last point in favor of skilletry: like all the "now cuisine," it's vitality food. Vitamins are retained, fat content is low, and the natural good taste of good food is heightened with this new-old cookery method that has found favor with good cooks across the country.

Hachis de Boeuf Diable

(Deviled beef with flageolets)

2 Tbs. butter
1/4 cup chopped shallots
2 Tbs. brandy
1/4 cup water
1/2 tsp. salt
1/4 tsp. pepper
1 Tbs. Escoffier Sauce Diable
1 Tbs. Dijon mustard
1/2 cup fine, dry bread crumbs
1 lb. lean sirloin beef, ground
1 Tbs. oil
1 Tbs. butter
2 Tbs. more brandy
1 (1-lb.) can flageolets (imported white beans)
2 more Tbs. Escoffier Sauce Diable
1/2 cup finely minced parsley

In a skillet, sauté shallots over medium heat until soft. Remove skillet from heat; add brandy, water, salt, pepper, Sauce Diable, and mustard. Blend, stir in bread crumbs. Add meat; mix well and shape into four patties. Heat oil with remaining butter in heavy skillet over medium high heat. Add meat patties and cook, turning once or twice, until crusty brown on both sides. Pour in brandy and ignite. Remove skillet from heat until flame subsides, add flageolets and liquid from can. Add remaining Sauce Diable; stir gently to mix beans with sauce. Return skillet to heat and cover; cook 5 to 10 minutes until meat is cooked through center and beans are hot. Stir in parsley and serve at once. *(See Menu Suggestion on p. 88.)*
   • *Makes 4 servings.*

MENU
SUGGESTION

Hachis de Boeuf Diable
French Bread
Red Bordeaux
Four-Minute Strawberry Cream (see p. 151)
Coffee

Skillet Steak with Peppers

All this requires for a superb meal is a glass of red wine;
for dessert, try the apple crumb bake on page 162.

1 lb. beef round steak
2 Tbs. peanut oil
1 clove garlic, peeled, minced
1 small white onion, peeled, minced
2 medium tomatoes, skinned, chopped
3 medium green peppers, seeded, cut into strips
1 (1-lb.) can tomato sauce
½ cup beef stock or water
2–3 dashes Tabasco sauce
½ tsp. sugar
Salt
Coarsely ground black pepper
3 cups cooked rice

Cut meat diagonally across the grain into thin strips.

In a large skillet heat the oil and quickly brown the meat in it. Add garlic and onion; stir-fry briefly. Add green-pepper strips, fresh tomatoes, and tomato sauce. Season with Tabasco, sugar, salt, and pepper. Partially cover skillet, let simmer 20 minutes or until meat is tender. Serve over rice.

• *Makes 4 servings.*

Bâttonets of Beef with Chive-and-Lemon Butter

Serve this over stir-fried broccoli and rice.

To complete a meal here just add an interesting bread, a glass of red wine, and a dessert. Fresh lemon ice cream would be perfect.

> 4 fillet steaks cut from end of whole fillet of beef; about ¾ inch thick, trimmed of all fat, gristle, and membrane
> Oil
> Salt
> Pepper
> 4 Tbs. chive and lemon butter *(see p. 90)*
> Stir-fried broccoli and rice *(see below)*

Cut each fillet across into strips about ¾ inch wide. Cover bottom of a heavy skillet with a very thin film of oil, place over medium heat. Sprinkle fillet strips lightly with salt and pepper. When the oil is very hot add them to the skillet and sauté very briefly, about 1 minute on each side, until browned but still rare in the center. Add the chive and lemon butter. When butter has melted, arrange the bâtonnets (4 to 5 strips per serving) over servings of broccoli and rice. Pour some of the butter sauce over each serving.

Broccoli and rice

> 1 bunch fresh broccoli
> 2 Tbs. butter
> 1 Tbs. lemon juice
> 4 cups cooked rice

Cut flowerets (tops) from broccoli stalks; trim stalks, cutting first across, then into "matchsticks" about 1 inch long. Place with flowerets in a large pan of heavily salted water, soak 5 minutes, drain, rinse with clear water. Steam over simmering water for 2 to 3 minutes or until just slightly tender. Heat the butter in a large skillet, add the broccoli, and stir-cook over medium heat until no raw taste remains. Add lemon juice, season lightly with salt. Add rice and stir-fry until heated.

Chive and lemon butter
>   1 tsp. minced chives
>   1 Tbs. lemon juice
>   4 Tbs. butter, at room temperature

Combine ingredients, blend well, Let stand about 1 hour to blend flavors.

Skilletry Beef Burgundy

All this noble dish needs is perhaps a bit of greenery, say, Bibb lettuce with a trace of dressing. For dessert, any of the ice creams in this book, and of course coffee.

>   4 1½-inch thick fillets of beef, at room temperature
>   1 Tbs. vegetable oil
>   2 Tbs. brandy
>   4 thick slices French-style bread
>   ½ lb. large mushrooms, trimmed, cut into thin,
>   T-shaped slices
>   1 tsp. minced shallots or green onion
>   2 Tbs. butter
>   ½ tsp. flour
>   1 more Tbs. butter, at room temperature
>   2 Tbs. Escoffier Sauce Diable (or other thick steak sauce)
>   Salt
>   Pepper

Flatten each fillet slightly by pounding once or twice with side of a heavy cleaver.

In a heavy skillet, heat the oil to almost smoking; add fillets and sear quickly on each side. Reduce heat; cook, turning once, 3 to 4 minutes. Increase heat, pour in brandy, and ignite. Remove skillet from heat until flame subsides.

Place bread slices on serving plates, top each with a fillet; set aside and keep warm.

Pour cooking oil from skillet, add butter, place over medium heat. Add mushrooms and shallots, sauté until tender, about 3 minutes. Pour in wine, cook over high heat until reduced to about half. Stir flour into remaining butter. Add to mushroom mixture; cook, stirring constantly, about 30 seconds. Add Sauce Diable, stir to blend. Season with salt and pepper (go easy on the salt; steak sauce is salty). Spoon sauce over fillets and bread. Serve at once.

• *Makes 4 servings.*

Skilletry Ginger Pork with Pineapple and Green Pepper

Add a dessert, perhaps slices of Southern Applesauce Cake.
Coffee, of course, and dinner is served.

1 lb. pork (with a little fat), cut into 1-inch cubes
Water
1 Tbs. oil
1 clove garlic, peeled, crushed
1 (1-inch) cube ginger root, crushed
1 green pepper, seeded, cut into strips
1 medium-size mild purple onion, peeled, chopped
½ cup chicken broth
¼ cup soy sauce
¼ cup sherry
¼ cup unsweetened pineapple juice, from 8-oz. can
     pineapple chunks
1 (8-oz.) can unsweetened pineapple chunks, drained
Hot cooked brown rice

Put pork cubes in a large deep skillet; add water to cover, bring to a boil. Lower heat, simmer until water evaporates. Stir cubes until lightly browned; remove from skillet, set aside. Add oil, garlic, ginger root, green pepper, and onion to skillet. Cook, stirring, 2 to 3 minutes; remove and discard garlic and ginger root. Return meat to skillet; add broth, soy sauce, sherry, and pineapple juice; simmer covered for about 15 minutes. Add pineapple chunks, cook a final 2 or 3 minutes. Serve over rice.

• *Makes 4 servings.*

Pork Chop Skillet Supper

Corn bread, hot and fragrant with plenty of butter, is a natural with pork chops. Add cold beer and follow with apples and cheese for dessert.

4 lean pork chops
1 Tbs. oil
½ cup dry sherry
¼ cup soy sauce
1 Tbs. minced fresh ginger *(optional)*
Sprinkling of coarsely ground black pepper
1½ cups chicken broth
2 carrots, scraped, cut in 1-inch slices
4 very small white onions, peeled
1 small head cabbage, trimmed, quartered

In a deep heavy skillet brown chops in oil over high heat. Pour off and discard any rendered fat and remaining oil. Add sherry, soy sauce, ginger, and pepper. Cover skillet, reduce heat, and let simmer until sherry has evaporated. Add salt, pepper, chicken broth, carrot slices, and onions, pushing carrots and onions into liquid around chops. Cover and simmer 20 to 25 minutes or until vegetables are tender. Add cabbage wedges, placing them on top of meat and other vegetables. Cover and cook until cabbage has lost its raw taste but is still slightly crisp.

• *Makes 4 servings.*

Skillet Pork in Sweet-and-Sour Sauce with Green Peppers and Tomatoes

Ice-cold beer tastes great with this combination of flavors.

2 large tomatoes
1 fillet of pork (1 to 1½ lbs.)
½ cup boiling water
2 Tbs. peanut oil
1 medium-size green pepper, seeded, cut into
   1 × ½-inch strips
3 Tbs. water
Sweet-and-sour sauce *(see below)*
3 to 4 cups hot cooked rice

Sweet-and-sour sauce

1½ Tbs. sugar
2 Tbs. white wine vinegar
4 Tbs. catsup
Juice from one orange (about ⅓ cup)
1 tsp. cornstarch
½ cup water

Cut tomatoes in halves; gently squeeze out seeds and juice. Cut halves into 1 × ½-inch strips. Set aside.

Cut fillet into thin slices (this is done easily if you place the meat in the freezer until very cold and firm but not frozen).

Place pork slices in a large skillet over high heat; add boiling water, lower heat, cover. Let simmer until water has evaporated. Remove meat, set aside. Wipe skillet thoroughly dry; pour in oil, place over high heat. Add green pepper strips. Cook and stir-fry 1 minute. Add pork slices and tomato strips. Stir 30 seconds, add water. Cover and steam about 1 minute. Uncover and stir 30 seconds. Stir in sweet-and-sour sauce. Gently toss and turn ingredients to coat with sauce. Cook a few seconds more, until the sauce thickens. Spoon over cooked rice. *(For preparing the sauce, see p. 94.)*

• *Makes 4 servings.*

To prepare Sweet-and-Sour Sauce

Combine ingredients in a small nonmetal bowl; beat with a whisk, until well blended.

Skillet Curried Pork with Cabbage

1½ lbs. lean pork tenderloin, cut into 1 × ¼-inch strips
1 clove garlic, peeled, crushed
1 bay leaf
2 Tbs. cider vinegar
½ tsp. salt
¼ tsp. coarsely ground black pepper
Boiling water
1 Tbs. butter
1 Tbs. vegetable oil
2 small white onions, peeled, minced
2 tart cooking apples, peeled, cored, and minced
1 Tbs. curry powder
1½ cups chicken stock or broth
1 cup shredded green cabbage
½ cup (bottled) chutney
Salt to taste
1 Tbs. cornstarch dissolved in 3 Tbs. hot water *(optional)*
3 cups hot cooked rice

Put pork strips in skillet with garlic, bay leaf, vinegar, salt, and pepper. Add boiling water sufficient to cover meat. Simmer, covered, until water evaporates and the pork begins to produce some fat for frying. Remove and discard garlic and bay leaf. Stir-fry meat until browned; remove with slotted spoon to a warm bowl. Add butter and oil to skillet; when butter is melted add onion and apple. Cook, stirring often, over low heat until apple is very soft.

Stir in curry powder. Add stock. Return meat to skillet, partially cover, and simmer 15 to 20 minutes. Stir in cabbage and chutney. Cover and cook until cabbage is tender but still slightly crisp, about 5 minutes. If desired, thicken sauce with cornstarch dissolved in water. Serve on rice.

• *Makes 4 servings.*

MENU
SUGGESTION

Skillet Curried Pork
with Cabbage
Chutney
Cold Beer
Fresh Lemon Ice Cream
Coffee

Skillet Chicken with Broccoli and Rice Piquant

Serve this elegant dish with a chilled dry white wine. Dessert
might be the Apricot Crème on page 160.

2 whole chicken breasts, skinned and boned
1 (10-oz.) package frozen chopped broccoli
2 Tbs. butter
2 Tbs. water
4 more Tbs. butter
Juice from 1 large lemon
Salt
Pepper
2 more Tbs. butter
3 cups cooked rice
½ cup slivered almonds
½ cup raisins
1 tsp. Dijon (or similar) mustard
1 Tbs. apple jelly
2 Tbs. very hot water

Split each chicken breast to make 4 "cutlets"; place between
sheets of waxed paper. Pound to ¼- to ½-inch thickness.

Remove frozen broccoli from package; let stand at room
temperature until thawed but still cold. In a large skillet, over
medium high heat, add the 2 Tbs. butter. When the butter foams,
add broccoli. Cook, stirring, for 1 minute. Add water; cover and
steam until broccoli is tender, about 5 minutes. Transfer to a
warm bowl. Melt the 4 Tbs. butter in same skillet, add chicken

cutlets, and sauté until firm and white through centers and lightly browned. Sprinkle with lemon juice, salt, and pepper. Arrange down the center of a large oval serving dish. Add remaining butter, rice, almonds, and raisins to skillet. Stir gently until grains of rice are coated with butter. Stir mustard into jelly, stir in hot water; add to skillet. Use a spatula to gently lift and stir mixture until evenly blended. Add cooked broccoli; stir and lift until mixed with rice and heated. Spoon around chicken breasts and serve at once.

- *Makes 4 servings.*

Poulet Sauté Riviera

(Skillet chicken with vegetables)

Crusty rolls are a must with this, as is a glass of dry white wine. For dessert, Poppy-Seed Cake (see p. 147), well sprinkled with rum and served with black coffee.

3 medium zucchini, trimmed
1 small mild purple onion, peeled
1 small green pepper, seeded
4 stalks celery
4 sprigs parsley
1 small jar pimiento-stuffed green olives
3 large ripe tomatoes, peeled
2 Tbs. oil
2 Tbs. sweet butter
¼ tsp. mixed Italian herbs*
½ tsp. salt
½ cup dry white wine
1 (3-lb.) chicken cut into 8 pieces: 2 wings, 2 legs,
    2 thighs, and breast cut into 2 halves

Coarsely chop zucchini, onion, green pepper, and celery in food processor or on chopping board with knife. Finely mince parsley; cut olives in half. Coarsely chop tomatoes. Heat oil

---

*Mixed Italian herbs are sold under various labels and often referred to as Italian seasoning.

and butter in a large heavy skillet; add all vegetables and cook over low heat, stirring occasionally, for about 15 minutes. Stir in seasoning and wine. Place chicken pieces over vegetables. Bring liquid to boil. Cover skillet with a sheet of aluminum foil and a tight-fitting lid. Place in a preheated 350° F. oven and bake for about 1 hour or until chicken is tender.

• *Makes 4 servings.*

Virginia Skillet Chicken with Ham

This is such an elegant dish it could be the star of a party buffet.

1 (10-oz.) package frozen lima beans
1 (10-oz.) package frozen sliced okra
2 Tbs. butter
2 Tbs. oil
¼ cup thinly sliced celery
½ cup chopped green onion
½ cup chopped green pepper
1 cup chopped lean cooked ham (preferably baked ham)
4 medium to large tomatoes, peeled and chopped
½ cup chicken stock or broth
1 Tbs. tomato puree or catsup
1 (10-oz.) package frozen kernel corn
1½ to 2 cups poached chicken, skinned and boned,
    cut into bite-size pieces
Salt
Pepper
Tabasco sauce
Cooked rice or fresh, hot corn-bread squares

Remove frozen beans and okra from packages; let stand at room temperature until thawed but still cold. In a large deep skillet melt butter with oil over medium heat. Add celery, onion, green pepper, and ham; sauté until vegetables are limp. Add tomatoes, lima beans, okra, and stock. Cover skillet; simmer until tomatoes are very soft and vegetables are cooked. Stir in tomato puree or catsup. Add corn and chicken; cook, stirring frequently, 2 or 3 minutes. Season with salt, pepper, and Tabasco sauce. Serve over rice or corn bread.

• *Makes about 6 to 8 servings.*

Skillet Deviled Chicken with Peas and Mushrooms

Honey, serve up the hot biscuits and make a batch of iced tea, for the best Deep-South supper ever.

1 (10-oz.) package frozen tiny green peas
8 to 12 large mushrooms
2 whole chicken breasts, skinned and boned
1 Tbs. vegetable oil
2 Tbs. butter
2 Tbs. dry sherry
2 Tbs. chicken stock or water
2 Tbs. Escoffier Sauce Diable, or substitute 2 Tbs. Heinz 57
  Sauce plus 1 tsp. Dijon or other hot mustard
Salt
Pepper
Hot cooked rice or flat noodles

Place frozen peas in a colander, hold under hot running tap water. Lift and toss gently with your fingers until peas are thawed and warm to the touch. Trim mushroom stems, remove from caps, and chop. Slice mushroom tops across into thin slices. Cut chicken breasts into bite-size cubes.

Heat oil with butter in skillet over medium heat. When butter has melted add chicken cubes; sauté until firm and white. Add mushroom stems; cook, stirring, about 1 minute. Add frozen peas and mushroom caps. Pour in sherry and stock or water. Cover and steam about 1 minute, or until peas are tender. Stir in Sauce Diable. Season with salt and pepper. Cook, stirring, a final 30 seconds. Serve over rice or noodles.

• *Makes 4 servings.*

Crabmeat Royale

*A truly elegant and luxurious dish to prepare when you feel
like indulging yourself. Deserves a glass of champagne; you
might add a salad of ripe honeydew melon slices lavishly
sprinkled with parsley, and hot Parker House rolls. For
dessert? Ripe fruit (peaches would be perfect) splashed with
cognac a few minutes before serving.*

1 lb. crabmeat
¼ lb. fresh mushrooms, trimmed, chopped
1 Tbs. minced green onion
4 Tbs. butter
¼ cup dry sherry
½ tsp. dry mustard
1 tsp. Worcestershire sauce
¾ cup heavy cream
2 egg yolks
¼ cup more heavy cream
Salt
Pepper
Grated Gruyère cheese *(optional)*

Remove cartilage from crabmeat. In large skillet sauté mushrooms and green onion in butter over moderate heat until soft.
Add crabmeat. Pour in sherry, add mustard, Worcestershire
sauce, and the ¾ cup of cream. Cook, stirring gently, until
heated. Beat egg yolks into remaining cream, add to crabmeat
mixture; stir until sauce thickens. Season to taste with salt and
pepper. Serve over toast or pour mixture into individual shells
or ramekins (or 1-qt. casserole dish); sprinkle with grated
cheese. Bake at 350° F. until cheese melts, about 5 minutes.
• *Makes 4 to 6 servings.*

Jambalaya

Jambalaya needs no embellishments to make a complete and perfect meal. French bread, of course, a glass of dry white wine, and a simple dessert are all that's needed or wanted.

1½ slices bacon
2 stalks celery, thinly sliced
½ small green pepper, seeded, chopped
1 medium-size mild purple onion, peeled, chopped
1 clove garlic, peeled, minced
6 large, ripe and juicy tomatoes, chopped
1 cup chicken stock
1 Tbs. tomato puree
Dash of Tabasco sauce
1 bay leaf
Kosher salt
Coarsely ground black Java pepper
1 lb. raw shrimp, peeled and deveined
2 cups diced cooked chicken
1 pt. oysters, drained *(optional)*
Cooked brown rice

In a large, deep heavy skillet cook bacon over low heat until all fat has been rendered and bacon is crisp. Remove bacon, crumble, set aside. Add celery, green pepper, onion, and garlic to fat in pan; cook, stirring, until vegetables are soft. Add tomatoes, stock, tomato puree, Tabasco, and bay leaf; season with salt and pepper. Partially cover skillet and let mixture simmer for about one hour or until reduced to a thick sauce. Add shrimp and chicken, let simmer until shrimp turns pink. If desired add oysters, cooking until edges curl. Spoon over rice. Sprinkle with reserved bacon, serve from the skillet.

• *Makes 6 to 8 servings.*

Hot Bean Salad

*A great dish to serve with cold "deli" corned beef. Add a
good mustard and ice-cold beer—it's a superb meal.*

1 lb. fresh green beans or 1 (10-oz.) package frozen
   green beans, thawed
1 (10-oz.) package frozen lima beans, thawed
4 slices bacon
1 medium-size mild purple onion, peeled, thinly sliced,
   slices broken into rings
1 (1-lb.) can kidney beans, drained
2 Tbs. sugar
2 Tbs. white wine vinegar
1 tsp. salt
¼ tsp. coarsely ground black pepper

If using fresh green beans, trim the beans, pinching off the tips
at both ends; break into 2-inch lengths. Rinse and drain, set
aside.

Place bacon in a large skillet over medium heat. Fry, turning
occasionally, until crisp. Transfer to paper toweling; drain,
crumble, set aside. Add green beans, lima beans, and onion to
rendered fat in skillet. Cover and cook over low heat, shaking
the skillet frequently. Cook about 10 minutes or until beans are
tender. Add remaining ingredients. Stir to blend; cook until
mixture is heated. Stir in crumbled bacon.

   • *Makes 6 to 8 servings.*

Flageolets à la Bretonne

(Flageolets and rice with tomatoes and ham)

All that's needed to complete this country French meal is some crusty bread, a mellow red wine, and a creamy, ripe cheese for dessert.

2 Tbs. butter
¼ cup minced green onion
2 large, very ripe and juicy fresh tomatoes,
    peeled and chopped
1 cup chopped lean baked ham
1 Tbs. tomato puree
3 cups canned flageolets (imported white beans)
Salt
Pepper
3 cups cooked brown rice *(see p. 84)*
½ cup minced parsley

Melt the butter in a large heavy skillet, add the green onion; sauté until soft. Add the tomatoes; cook, stirring and chopping the tomatoes with the tip of a spatula, until reduced to a coarse sauce. (If tomatoes are not sufficiently juicy, add a little water or liquid from flageolets.) Add ham, stir in tomato puree. Add beans, season lightly with salt (remember, ham is salty) and pepper. Cook, stirring gently, until beans are heated. Spoon over rice, sprinkle with minced parsley. Serve very hot.

• *Makes about 4 servings.*

Cuban Red Beans and Rice Supper

Beer is the classic drink with this traditional Cuban dish. For dessert, try broiled bananas flamed with a little rum and brown sugar.

1 lb. lean pork, cut into small cubes
Water
1 clove garlic, peeled and minced

 1 large onion, peeled, chopped
1 (4-oz.) can chopped green chilies, drained
1 cup chicken broth or stock (or water)
1 (1-lb.) can Italian-style tomato sauce
4 cups red beans, canned or home cooked
Salt
Coarsely ground black pepper
2 barely ripe bananas
1 (8-oz.) can pineapple cubes
1 small head Boston lettuce, shredded
Cooked brown rice *(see p. 84)*

Put pork in a large deep skillet. Add water to cover, simmer until water evaporates. Add garlic and onion; cook, stirring, until vegetables and pork cubes are lightly browned. Add chicken broth and tomato sauce; let simmer about 30 minutes. Stir in beans, simmer about 20 minutes longer. Season with salt and pepper. Add bananas and pineapple; cook a final 2 or 3 minutes. Stir in lettuce; spoon over rice and serve immediately.

    • *Makes about 6 servings.*

Lentils, Brazilian Style

Beer (the light imported variety, served icy cold) is the beverage; the accompaniment—black bread and butter.

 2 cups lentils
Water
1 (4-oz.) can chopped green chilies, drained
¼ lb. prosciutto (or other smoked ham), thinly sliced, slices cut into slivers
Coarsely ground black pepper *(optional)*
Salt *(optional)*
1 small head Boston lettuce, trimmed and shredded
2 or 3 large navel oranges, peeled, cut into thick slices
Cooked brown rice *(see p. 84)*

Put lentils in a large heavy skillet, add water to cover by about 1 inch; add green chilies and ham. Bring to boil, lower heat. Let simmer until lentils are tender and almost all water is absorbed, about 45 minutes (add additional water if necessary as lentils cook). Taste, season with pepper and with salt if desired (prosciutto is salty, and additional salt is rarely needed). If too much liquid remains, remove ¼ to ½ cup of lentils and puree in blender (or mash to a paste with a fork); stir this back into beans to thicken liquid.

To serve, arrange portions of lentils, shredded lettuce, orange slices, and rice separately like 4 spokes of a wheel on each serving plate. Lentils and rice should be very hot; lettuce and orange at room temperature.

  • *Makes about 6 generous servings.*

★

Mixed Vegetable Sauté

Try this with room-temperature Southern fried chicken—add currant jelly and hot rolls for a Down-South supper.

    4 medium carrots
    2 medium zucchini
    2 medium cucumbers
    2 Tbs. butter
    3 Tbs. water
    2 more Tbs. butter
    Salt
    Coarsely ground pepper

Trim and scrape the carrots; cut into the thinnest possible slices. The easiest way to do this, of course, is by using a food processor with slicing disk. Lacking a processor, use a French *mandoline,* if you have one, or your wooden chopping board and a sharp knife. Trim and thinly slice the zucchini by whatever method you are using. Peel the cucumbers, cut them in half lengthwise, and with a small sharp spoon scoop out and discard the seeds; cut the halves into thin slices.

Melt 2 Tbs. of butter in a skillet, add the carrot slices, and sauté over medium heat for about 5 minutes. Add the water, bring to a boil, cover the skillet, and let the carrots steam for about 3 minutes or until almost all the water has evaporated. Add the zucchini, cucumber, and remaining butter. Sauté the vegetables for 2 or 3 minutes, cover, and let steam about 2 minutes. Then uncover and continue to sauté until they are tender but not overcooked. Season with salt and pepper.

• *Makes 4 to 6 servings.*

NOTE: If you like, stir 1 cup cold cooked rice into the cooked vegetables and continue to cook, stirring gently, until rice is heated.

★

Creole Vegetables

One of the best "fresh and frozen" combinations and one of the most versatile. Served over hot corn-bread squares with a slice of cold boiled or baked ham on the plate, it's a meal to remember.

1 Tbs. oil
2 Tbs. butter
1 medium-size mild purple onion, peeled, chopped
1 small green pepper, seeded, chopped
2 stalks celery, trimmed, cut diagonally into very thin slices
2 large ripe tomatoes, skinned, chopped
1 tsp. sugar
½ tsp. salt
Coarsely ground black pepper
1 (10-oz.) package frozen lima beans
1 (10-oz.) package frozen okra
Water
1 (10-oz.) package frozen kernel corn
2 Tbs. catsup

Heat oil and butter in a large skillet; add onion, green pepper, and celery; cook, stirring, 2 to 3 minutes. Add tomatoes; continue to cook and stir over fairly high heat until tomatoes are reduced to a chunky sauce. Stir in sugar, salt, and a generous amount of pepper; add frozen lima beans and okra. Add ¼ to ½ cup water (less if tomatoes are very ripe and juicy, more if they are under-ripe, with insufficient juice). Cover skillet and let mixture simmer until beans and okra are tender, about 10 minutes. Stir occasionally and add a little more water if mixture becomes dry. Add corn, stir in catsup. Cover and let steam 2 to 3 minutes.

  • *Makes 6 to 8 servings.*

Sicilian Caponata

Serve as an appetizer or a light lunch. In either case, add some crusty French bread and a light dry wine; a Beaujolais would be perfect.

  1 small (1 lb. or a bit less) eggplant
  2 Tbs. salt
  1 large tomato
  4 Tbs. oil
  1 small clove garlic, peeled, minced
  1 small onion, peeled, finely chopped
  2 small zucchini, trimmed, thinly sliced
  2 stalks celery, thinly sliced
  ½ cup water
  1 Tbs. tomato paste
  ⅓ cup red wine vinegar
  1 (6-oz.) can pitted black olives
  1 (2½-oz.) can rolled, caper-stuffed anchovies, drained and
    blotted with paper toweling to remove excess oil
  1 tsp. dried oregano
  Freshly ground black pepper
  Salt *(optional)*

Trim eggplant, cut into ½-inch slices. Cut each slice into 4 wedges; place in a colander, sprinkle with salt, let drain 30 minutes. Rinse with cold water, blot dry.

Plunge tomato into boiling water, hold under cold water, slip off skin. Cut in half, gently squeeze halves to remove almost all seeds; coarsely chop.

Heat oil in a large skillet. Add garlic and onion; sauté until tender, about 5 minutes. Add eggplant, tomato, zucchini, and celery. Cook, stirring over medium heat, 3 to 4 minutes. Add water, cover, and let steam until no raw taste remains in vegetables but they are still slightly crisp, about 5 minutes. Stir tomato paste into vinegar, pour into skillet, add olives and anchovies; mix gently with a spatula. Continue to cook 2 to 3 minutes. Cover and let steam a final 1 to 2 minutes. Don't overcook. Add oregano and a generous grinding of pepper. Taste and add salt. (The anchovies are salty, so go easy here.) Stir in parsley just before serving.

NOTES: Serve hot or at room temperature. Caponata can be made ahead of time; the flavors improve by "standing." Refrigerate if not served within an hour after cooking, but for best flavor do bring at least partially to room temperature before serving. It will "keep" covered in the refrigerator up to a week. Leftovers can be served as an appetizer or relish.

Mexican Skillet Vegetables

Try this with thin slices of cold roast beef and a very special dessert, say, peanut butter cake with burnt-sugar ice cream.

2 Tbs. peanut or safflower oil
1 small clove garlic, peeled, crushed
1 small white onion, peeled, chopped
½ small green pepper, seeded, chopped
2 medium yellow squash, trimmed, sliced
2 medium zucchini, trimmed, sliced
2 Tbs. water
1½ cups fresh corn kernels or 1 (10-oz.) package
 frozen corn kernels
1 tsp. sugar
2 to 3 tsp. chili powder
1 tsp. salt
Freshly ground black pepper

Heat oil with garlic in a large skillet over medium heat until garlic browns. Remove and discard garlic; add onion and green pepper to skillet. Cook, stirring, 1 to 2 minutes. Add squash, zucchini, and water. Cover and cook over low heat for 20 minutes or until vegetables are tender. Add sugar, chili powder, and salt. Gently lift and stir vegetables to mix in seasoning. Add pepper to taste.

• *Makes 4 to 6 servings.*

Skillet Vegetable Curry

This is an especially good dish to serve with leftover cold turkey. For dessert, raspberry sorbet makes a perfect ending.

2 Tbs. butter
1 Tbs. mild oil
1 small onion, peeled, chopped
1 small green pepper, seeded and chopped
4 stalks celery, trimmed, thinly sliced
2 small tart apples, peeled, cored, and chopped
1 Tbs. curry powder
1 small head cabbage, shredded
Salt
¼ cup water
3 to 4 cups cooked rice
1 cup chopped dry-roasted peanuts

Melt butter with oil in a large deep skillet; add onion, green pepper, celery, and apple. Cook, stirring, until vegetables are soft, about 5 minutes. Stir in curry powder, add cabbage, salt to taste, and water. Stir to combine ingredients. Cover and cook over medium heat until cabbage loses its raw taste but is still crisp, about 10 minutes. Serve over hot rice, sprinkling each serving with chopped peanuts.

• *Makes about 6 servings.*

Corn Tomato Rarebit

A lovely summer lunch; follow with fresh peaches and sour cream, dusted with brown sugar.

3 Tbs. butter
1 small onion, peeled, chopped
4 large tomatoes, peeled
2 cups fresh (or frozen) corn kernels
Salt
½ lb. soft cheddar cheese, crumbled
Thin crisp toast

Melt the butter in a heavy skillet. Add the onion and sauté until soft; add tomatoes and cook over medium heat, chopping them still more until they are reduced to a chunky sauce. Add the corn; cook, stirring, for about 1 minute. Season with salt. Stir in the cheese. When cheese has melted, spoon mixture over thin, crisp toast and serve at once.
  • *Makes about 4 servings.*

Frittata

This dish is very easy to make; serve it with a well-seasoned tomato sauce spooned over as a main course for lunch or supper. It is also good cold, sliced in thin wedges, and served as an hors d'oeuvre. It can be made with string beans instead of the green peas; cooked cubes of zucchini can replace the potatoes; and crisp, cooked crumbled bacon can be used instead of the ham, In other words, it's what I call a "loose" recipe: use what you have on hand, use your imagination.

2 Tbs. butter
1 Tbs. mild oil
1 small onion, peeled, finely minced
2 small cooked potatoes, chilled, peeled, and chopped
½ cup cooked green peas
½ cup chopped baked or boiled ham
4 eggs beaten with 1 Tbs. water and seasoned lightly with
   salt, pepper, and a sprinkling of oregano
1 Tbs. grated Parmesan or Romano cheese

Preheat oven broiler. Put butter with oil in a 10-inch skillet with a heatproof handle. Place over medium heat, add the onion, and cook, stirring, 1 minute. Add potatoes, stir until heated and flecked with brown; add the peas and ham, stir 30 seconds. Pour in the beaten, seasoned eggs; do not stir but slide the skillet back and forth over the heat for a few seconds. When the bottom of the frittata is set and firm (to test, lift edge gently with a spatula), sprinkle the top with the grated cheese; place in the oven, about 4 inches under high broiler heat, until well puffed and lightly browned. Cut into wedges and serve hot or at room temperature.

  • *Makes 4 main-course servings; serves 8 to 10 as an hors d'oeuvre.*

MENU
SUGGESTION

Frittata
Cold Sliced Tomatoes
(sprinkled with salt, pepper, and a trace of sugar)
Bourbon Apples (see p. 156)
Coffee

Slow-Cooked Meals

WONDER OF WONDERS—deep-down, slow-cooked flavor is back, but it's back without deep-down slow hours in the kitchen. Perhaps the most popular of all the new appliances to be developed within the last few years, the slow-cooking pot has won the most favor with the most people. Try it, you'll like it; that expression was probably coined for the slow-cooking pot.

For here is truly the work-saving, time-saving appliance that delivers the goods; it also has the pleasant quality of being relatively inexpensive. Now if this seems like excessive praise, it isn't, for after you try a few recipes in the slow cooker you really will, as the ads say, wonder how you did without it. For truth to tell, no matter how "au courant" you may be about the new food and the new cooking methods, there comes a time when only a "dishy dish," as my British friends would call it, will do. Meaning, of course, a dish that combines a number of flavoring ingredients and is then slow cooked to a mellow blend of taste and texture. An impossible feat in fast cooking and, until the advent of the electric slow cooker, a tedious task of stirring and watching, testing and tasting. But no longer. You can have your "dishy dish" and your freedom too; truly the kitchen revolution has freed the slaves. Moreover, your slow-cooked dish is a meal in itself in genuine new-style cookery fashion. All that's needed is to serve the star attraction with good bread and some good wine, and hopefully to finish the meal with the civilized pleasure of dessert and coffee.

Smothered Steak, Slightly Italian Style

Like all our slow-cooked dishes, this needs only a salad, perhaps Italian rugola, to keep the Roman style.

1½ to 2 lbs. round steak
2 Tbs. flour
1 tsp. salt
⅛ tsp. pepper
2 Tbs. oil
1 (8-oz.) can tomato sauce
1 (8-oz.) can pizza sauce
1 (4½-oz.) jar chopped mushrooms, drained
Hot cooked thin spaghetti

Cut steak into serving-size pieces. Coat with flour, salt, and pepper; use the side of a heavy cleaver to pound the flour and seasoning into the meat. Heat the oil in a large heavy skillet or in slow-cooking pot with browning unit. Brown the meat in the hot oil, one or two pieces at a time. Combine meat and remaining ingredients in slow-cooking pot. Cover and cook on low 6 to 8 hours or until meat is tender. Serve with hot cooked thin spaghetti.

• *Makes 6 servings.*

Sauerbraten

Accompany with a platter of tomato slices vinaigrette and finish with apple crisp. Men especially love this menu.

3½ to 4 lbs. beef rump or sirloin tip
1 large onion, peeled, thinly sliced
1 cup water
1 cup cider vinegar
1 tsp. sugar
1 tsp. salt
6 whole peppercorns
1 Tbs. mixed pickling spices

¼ cup brown sugar, packed down
6 to 8 gingersnaps, crumbled
Hot cooked noodles

Put meat in a large (nonmetal) bowl, cover with onion slices. Combine water and vinegar in a saucepan, bring to a boil, add sugar, salt, peppercorns, and pickling spices; pour over meat and onions. Cover and refrigerate 24 to 36 hours; turn meat several times during marinating. Place meat in slow-cooking pot; pour one cup marinade over meat. Cover and cook on low 6 to 8 hours. Slice meat; place slices on a serving platter, keep warm. Strain meat juices, skim off fat. Put brown sugar in a heavy skillet over low heat. When it begins to melt, slowly add the strained cooking liquid, then the gingersnaps. Cook, stirring, until thick and smooth. Pour sauce over meat and serve immediately with hot cooked noodles.
  • *Makes 8 servings.*

Texas Pot Roast

Add a salad of crisp lettuce with poppy seed dressing, and dinner is served. This roast makes fabulous "letfovers," too.

3 to 3½ lbs. beef pot roast
Salt
Pepper
1 medium onion, peeled, sliced
½ cup chili sauce
2–3 dashes tabasco sauce
1 tsp. chili powder
1½ cups beer
Cooked noodles

Place meat in slow-cooking pot, sprinkle with salt and pepper. Combine remaining ingredients; blend and pour over meat. Cover and cook on low for 8 to 10 hours. Remove meat from pot. Let stand a few minutes before slicing. Pour cooking liquid from slow-cooking pot into a 10-inch skillet. Let stand a few minutes, then skim off fat; place skillet over medium heat until liquid has reduced to about half. Spoon over meat slices just before serving. Serve with hot, freshly cooked noodles.

• *Makes 6 to 8 servings.*

Texas Pot Roast with Beans

A great party meal: add a salad and an easy dessert, and the host or hostess will have as good a time as the guests.

    3½ to 4 lbs. beef pot roast
    2 Tbs. vegetable oil
    1 large onion, peeled, chopped
    1 clove garlic, peeled, minced
    1 tsp. salt
    ½ tsp. pepper
    1 (8-oz.) can tomato sauce
    ½ cup chili sauce
    ¼ cup cider vinegar
    2 tsp. brown sugar
    1 tsp. Worcestershire sauce
    ½ cup water
    1 Tbs. chili powder
    2 (1-lb.) cans kidney beans, drained well and rinsed

Blot meat dry. Heat oil in a heavy skillet to almost smoking. Add meat and brown well on all sides; drain and place in slow-cooking pot. (Or brown meat in slow-cooking pot with browning unit, then pour off excess fat.) Sprinkle meat with salt and pepper, top with onions and garlic. Combine remaining ingredients except beans, pour over meat. Cover and cook on low 6 to 8 hours or until meat is tender. Remove meat, slice, and keep warm. Add beans to cooking liquid. Cover and cook on high 15 to 20 minutes or until heated. Serve meat with beans; spoon sauce over all.

• *Makes 8 to 10 servings.*

Pot Roast, Italian Style

3 to 4 lbs. beef chuck roast
Salt
Pepper
1 tsp. mixed Italian herbs
1 large ripe tomato, chopped
1 (1-lb.) jar Italian-style cooking sauce with mushrooms
1 Tbs. red wine vinegar

Sprinkle meat with salt and pepper, then mixed herbs. Place in slow-cooking pot; top with chopped tomato. Combine cooking sauce and vinegar; pour over and around meat and tomatoes. Cover and cook on low 6 to 8 hours or until meat is tender.

• *Makes 6 servings.*

NOTE: For the best hot sandwich ever, slice meat and place on thick slices of Italian-style bread. Spoon sauce over both bread and meat.

Braised Deviled Beef

Serve hot or cold with thick-sliced country-style bread. Apples and cheese would be nice for dessert.

3 to 4 lbs. beef rump roast (or substitute beef chuck)
Salt
Pepper
Peanut oil
1 medium onion, peeled, chopped
1 medium carrot, scraped, chopped
1 stalk celery, chopped
2 cloves garlic, peeled, minced
1½ cups homemade beef stock, or water
2 Tbs. (bottled) Sauce Diable (or substitute other thick steak sauce)

Bring meat to room temperature, rub with salt and pepper. Heat a thin film of oil in a heavy frying pan. Add beef and brown on both sides. Put onion, carrot, celery, and garlic in slow-cooking pot; push vegetables together, and place meat over them. Add stock. Cover and cook on low for about 6 to 8 hours or until meat is tender. Remove meat from pot. Strain stock into a saucepan. Cook, stirring, over high heat until reduced by half. Stir in Sauce Diable or steak sauce. Correct seasoning with additional salt and pepper if desired. Slice meat, serve with a little sauce spooned over each serving.

NOTE: Small onions and carrots may be added to the pot with the stock and cooked with the meat.

Beef Stew, Home Style

Homemade bread and butter and a glass of red wine—what could be better?

> 2 lbs. beef stew meat, cut into 1-inch cubes
> Flour
> Salt
> Pepper
> 2 Tbs. oil
> 6 carrots, scraped, cut into thick slices
> 12 very small whole onions, peeled
> 2 (10½-oz.) cans beef broth
> 2 cups water
> 1 tsp. sugar
> 1 tsp. Worcestershire sauce
> 2–3 dashes Tabasco sauce
> 1 (10-oz.) package frozen green peas, partially thawed
> Bottled horseradish *(optional)*
> Sour cream *(optional)*

Blot meat dry, dredge with flour, season with salt and pepper. Press flour into meat; shake off excess. Heat oil in a large heavy skillet or slow-cooking pot with browning unit. Brown meat cubes in hot oil a few at a time, drain. In slow-cooking pot combine meat, carrots, and onions. Mix beef broth with water, sugar, Worcestershire sauce, and Tabasco; pour over meat and vegetables. Cover and cook on low about 8 hours or until meat and vegetables are tender. Turn control on high, add peas; cover and cook 10 to 15 minutes or until peas are tender. Add horseradish to taste if desired, and thicken sauce just before serving with sour cream.

   • *Makes 6 to 8 servings.*

Not-So-Classic Pot-au-Feu

In France, where this recipe originated, all that would be added would be good bread and good wine; a red Bordeaux is traditional.

3 medium white onions, peeled, quartered
6 small carrots, scraped
1 stalk celery, cut into 2-inch pieces
1 tsp. sugar
1 tsp. salt
Coarsely ground black pepper
1 (3- to 3½-lb.) piece of beef, rump or bottom round
5 cups homemade beef stock (or part canned beef stock, part water)
1 Tbs. vinegar
1 small head cabbage, cut into wedges

Sauce

1 cup reserved beef broth
1 small tart apple
2 Tbs. prepared horseradish
Salt to taste
Pepper

Place onions, carrots, and celery in slow-cooking pot. Rub sugar, salt, and a liberal amount of pepper into surface of meat; place over vegetables. Add stock and vinegar. Cover pot and cook 5 to 7 hours or until meat is tender. (Just before last hour of cooking, remove 1 cup broth and place in a pan of ice water or in freezer to chill.) Remove meat to a warm serving platter. Turn heat to high, add cabbage to pot; cover and cook until no raw taste remains but cabbage is still crisp. While cabbage cooks, prepare sauce: Remove surface fat from cup of chilled reserved broth; place broth in container of food processor or electric blender. Add apple, blend to a thin puree; pour into a small saucepan. Add horseradish. Stir over medium heat until thickened and smooth. Season to taste with salt and pepper. Serve sauce with meat and vegetables.

• *Makes about 6 servings.*

NOTE: Pour any remaining broth into a storage bowl. Cover and refrigerate; when fat has risen to surface and congealed, remove and discard. Heat and serve broth as soup for another meal, or store in freezer to use when needed as stock.

Hungarian Goulash

Instead of a salad, why not fruit and cheese for dessert? A red wine would be perfect with both.

3 lbs. beef stew meat, cut into 1-inch cubes
½ cup flour
1 tsp. salt
¼ tsp. pepper
2 Tbs. oil
1 Tbs. paprika
1 large onion, peeled, chopped
1 clove garlic, peeled, minced
1 (8-oz.) can tomato sauce with mushrooms
1 Tbs. brown sugar
1½ tsp. dry mustard
Juice from 1 large lemon
1 cup beef stock or water
1 Tbs. butter, at room temperature
1 Tbs. flour
Hot cooked flat noodles or rice

Blot meat cubes dry, dredge with flour mixed with salt and pepper; press into cubes, shake off excess. Heat oil in a large skillet or slow-cooking pot with browning unit. Brown meat cubes, a few at a time, in the hot oil. Drain off excess fat. Sprinkle meat in slow-cooking pot with paprika, stirring and turning cubes to season evenly. Add onion and garlic. Combine tomato sauce, brown sugar, mustard, lemon juice, and beef stock or water; blend, pour over meat cubes. Cover and cook on low 6 to 8 hours or until meat is tender. Knead butter with flour to make a paste. Add to sauce; cook on high 10 to 15 minutes or until thickened. Serve over noodles or rice.

• *Makes 6 servings.*

Meatballs with Noodles

Serve this on a frosty night with crisp apples and a mellow cheese for dessert.

4 Tbs. butter
2 stalks celery, finely chopped
1 large onion, finely chopped
1 medium green pepper, finely chopped
1 Tbs. flour
1 (10½-oz.) can beef broth or stock
½ cup dry white wine
Salt
Pepper
3 slices white bread, crust removed
1 clove garlic, peeled, chopped
¾ lb. lean veal
¾ lb. cooked ham
¼ tsp. ground nutmeg
2 eggs
2 Tbs. more butter
2 Tbs. oil
½ cup lemon juice
½ cup grated Parmesan cheese
Hot just-cooked noodles

Melt the 4 Tbs. butter in a large skillet over medium heat. Add celery, onion, and green pepper. Sauté until onion is soft, about 10 minutes. Stir in flour. When blended, add beef broth and wine, simmer 2 minutes. Taste, add pepper, salt if necessary (if using canned broth, mixture is already salty), reserve.

Place bread in processor, process to fine crumbs. Remove bread crumbs, set aside. With motor running, add garlic, process until finely ground. Add meats, process until finely ground. Add nutmeg, eggs, and bread crumbs. Process until thoroughly blended. Remove from processor to mixing bowl and form into bite-size balls.

Without processor, make crumbs from bread slices in electric mixer or with hand grater; finely mince garlic. Grind meats through fine blade of meat grinder or have your butcher do this for you in advance. Combine bread crumbs, minced garlic, ground meats, and eggs in mixing bowl. Mix thoroughly with your hands. Shape into bite-size balls.

Brown meatballs, a few at a time, in remaining butter and oil over medium heat. When all are browned, transfer them to a slow-cooking pot; add reserved sauce. Cook on high heat 1 to 2 hours before serving; or on low heat until ready to serve, 6 to 8 hours.

Stir in lemon juice and sprinkle with Parmesan cheese just before serving. Serve over hot noodles.

• *Makes 4 to 6 servings.*

Yams 'n' Beans 'n' Ham You-All

This is so mouth-watering you need add only a glass of white wine plus a fresh-fruit dessert to make most people supremely happy.

2 large yams or sweet potatoes, peeled, very thinly sliced
½ lb. boiled or baked ham, cut into thin slices
1 (10-oz.) package frozen lima beans, thawed sufficiently
   to separate beans
¼ cup firmly packed light brown sugar
2 tsp. Dijon (or similar) mustard

1 tsp. curry powder
½ tsp. salt
1½ cups chicken broth or stock, heated to boiling

In slow-cooking pot layer yam slices, ham, and lima beans, beginning and ending with yams. Stir sugar, mustard, curry powder, and salt into boiling hot broth or stock. Pour into slow-cooking pot over yam and bean mixture. Cover and cook on low heat 6 to 8 hours.

• *Makes 6 servings.*

NOTE: If preferred, layer yam slices, ham, and beans in a Dutch oven, pour in liquid mixture, cover, and bake in 350° F. conventional oven for 1½ to 2 hours.

Spiced Corned Beef

Great to have on hand for an impromptu meal. Serve the meat at room temperature; add hot steamed new potatoes. Cook the cabbage at the last moment, either in reserved broth or in a steamer, as you prefer.

3 to 4 lbs. corned beef brisket
Water
1 large onion, peeled, chopped
1 clove garlic, peeled, minced
2 tsp. pickling spices
1 head cabbage, trimmed, cut into wedges *(optional)*

Place corned beef in slow-cooking pot. Barely cover with water. Add remaining ingredients. Cover and cook on low 10 to 12 hours.

If cabbage is included, lift cooked corned beef out of pot, turn control to high. Add cabbage wedges to corned beef broth; cover, cook 15 to 20 minutes or until cabbage has lost its raw taste but is still slightly crisp.

• *Makes 6 to 8 servings.*

Boiled Beef Tongue
(For some special eating)

Tiny new potatoes make a great "go with" for all three versions.

    1 (3½- to 4-lb.) beef tongue
    1½ quarts water
    1 clove garlic, peeled, crushed
    1 medium onion, peeled, chopped
    2 bay leaves
    1 cup cider vinegar
    1 tsp. mixed pickling spices

Combine all ingredients in a slow-cooking pot. Cover and cook on low 10 to 12 hours or until tongue is tender. Remove from pot, cool; with a small sharp knife, peel off the skin. Serve hot with sauce of your choice, or serve at room temperature with mustard and pickles, Cumberland sauce, horseradish and sour cream, or as you like it.

Variations

Glazed Tongue

    1 cup dry white wine
    ¼ cup honey
    1 tsp. cinnamon
    4 thin slices lemon, each cut into 4 wedges
    8 to 12 thin slices tongue

Combine wine, honey, cinnamon, and lemon slices in a nonmetal saucepan or skillet. Stir over medium heat until blended. Let simmer until mixture thickens slightly. Add tongue slices; turn and cook in the sauce until heated and glazed.

• *Makes 4 to 6 servings.*

Tongue with Spanish Sauce

    3 Tbs. butter
    1 clove garlic, peeled, minced
    1 large onion, peeled, chopped
    2 Tbs. flour
    1 cup dry white wine
    1 (8-oz.) can tomato sauce
    ½ cup sliced pimiento-stuffed olives
    8 to 12 thin slices boiled tongue, warm or at
        room temperature

Melt the butter in a deep 10-inch skillet, add garlic and onion; sauté over low heat until tender. Stir in flour; when blended, slowly add the wine, continuing to stir. Cook, stirring, until smooth; stir in tomato sauce. Continue to stir and cook until sauce is thickened. Stir in olives. Spoon over tongue slices and serve at once.

Stuffed Chicken

Stuffing

    1½ cups corn-bread stuffing mix (Pepperidge Farm brand)
    2 Tbs. frozen concentrated orange juice
    3 Tbs. butter
    1 small white onion, peeled, minced
    1 small tart apple, peeled, cored, finely chopped
    1 egg
    Dry white wine or water
    1 (4- to 5-lb.) roasting chicken
    2 medium carrots, peeled, sliced
    1 medium onion, peeled, chopped
    1 stalk celery, sliced
    Water
    Salt
    Pepper
    Paprika

In a mixing bowl, combine stuffing mix and orange juice. Melt butter in a small frying pan; add onion and apple. Cook, stirring, over low heat until onion is soft; add to dressing mixture. Stir in egg. Add enough wine or water to make a moist but still firm dressing. Rinse and dry chicken; stuff with dressing. Place carrots, onion, and celery in slow-cooking pot. Put chicken over vegetables; sprinkle with salt. Cover pot, cook on low for 6 to 8 hours or until chicken is tender. Sprinkle with paprika and serve; or, if desired, transfer chicken to a shallow roasting pan and brown in a preheated 450° F. oven 10 to 15 minutes.

• *Makes about 6 servings.*

MENU
SUGGESTION

Roast Stuffed Chicken with Dressing
Celery and Cucumber Sticks, Cherry Tomatoes
Dry White Wine
Cointreau Ice Cream
Coffee

White Beans with Garlic and Tomatoes

1 lb. dried white kidney, marrow, or navy beans
Water for soaking
4 cups water (approximately)
1 clove garlic, peeled, minced
1 stalk celery, chopped
2 or 3 large fresh tomatoes, quartered
1 tsp. salt
Coarsely ground black pepper

Put beans in electric slow-cooking pot; cover with water. Cook on high until water simmers; let simmer 30 minutes. Turn off heat, allow beans to soak uncovered for about 2 hours. Drain. Return beans to pot; add garlic, celery, and water to cover by about 1 inch. Cook on high heat for 1 to 2 hours; add tomatoes and salt. Cook on low heat until beans are tender. Cooking time varies according to age (and dryness) of beans: 4 to 6 hours is sufficient for most beans, but they may cook several hours longer in a slow-cooking pot without becoming too soft.

• *Makes about 8 cups.*

Variation

White Beans with Caviar

3 cups hot cooked white beans
3 cups hot, cooked, imported Italian short-grain rice
1 (3½-oz.) jar red lumpfish caviar

Serve very hot beans over freshly cooked, very hot rice. Sprinkle with chilled caviar and serve at once.

• *Makes 4 to 6 servings.*

NOTES: Instead of caviar, add about ¼ lb. thin strips of Smithfield or other smoked ham. Or serve hot beans with thinly sliced baked or boiled ham and add a spiced peach to each plate.

Pasta Meals

ONE OF THE PLEASURES OF THE NEW CUISINE is our newfound skill
with simple but superb meals, and nowhere is this more evident
than in America's romance with pasta. It is, in fact, one of the
most popular of foods, and when properly cooked and sauced,
is one of the most satisfyingly delicious of meals.

Proper cooking means freshly cooked—at the last moment—
pasta, plus a sauce that is inventive and super-delicious, yet
simple and easy.

Pasta meals call for no more than the main attraction, a good
bread, a robust wine, and fresh fruit for dessert. Such meals were
made in heaven, to be consumed with pleasure and lingered over
afterward with the unwinding companion of small cups of
black coffee.

Though the preparation time is no more than 30 minutes,
pasta meals were meant to be enjoyed at leisure. They are
indeed a civilized pleasure to enhance our sense of good living,
and isn't that what good food is all about?

ON COOKING PASTA

The purist (to put it politely) will tell you the only pasta worth
the boiling is that which you make yourself—from scratch.
Perhaps this is true: indeed pasta-making is relatively easy with
some of the pasta machines now on the market. If you like to
experiment in the kitchen, try it; you may like it. However, I
find many of the made-in-Italy pastas, along with one or two
domestic varieties (notably, for me, Buitoni), quite sufficient to
please my taste. Cooking pasta is another matter; here there are

126

rules—simple ones, but definite. No one can tell you how long to cook your pasta. Obviously, fine noodles or thin spaghetti are going to cook faster than macaroni; you simply have to test by tasting. Pasta is done when it loses its raw taste and is soft but still firm to the bite—al dente.

To cook pasta properly you need a large pot of rapidly boiling water into which you have stirred a tablespoon of salad oil and a small amount of salt. Use half the salt recommended on the package. Pasta should have a "gentle" taste: you want to taste the pasta, not the salt. Add the pasta gradually to the boiling water; the water should not stop boiling. Stir once, let boil 3 to 5 minutes depending on type, then start testing. When it is cooked to your satisfaction, empty into a large colander and rinse with very hot water. Melt a generous piece of butter in the cooking pot and return the pasta to it. Swirl the pasta around in the butter and serve immediately with very hot sauce. Or simply add a generous amount of finely minced parsley (a cupful for four servings is not too much), an equal amount of freshly grated Parmesan cheese, and, if desired, two or three tablespoons of heavy cream. Toss briefly and serve at once. If you like, peeled and seeded tomato strips (be sure they are at room temperature) may be added just before serving. It's a beautiful meal.

Pasta with Mushroom Sauce

A salad of Italian rugola would be a nice accompaniment, plus of course a red wine and good bread!

1 medium onion, peeled, finely chopped
½ lb. mushrooms, trimmed, sliced
6 Tbs. butter
¼ cup Marsala
Salt
Coarsely ground black pepper
¼ cup light cream, at room temperature
1 lb. thin spaghetti
¼ cup minced parsley
Grated Parmesan cheese

Sauté the onion and mushrooms in butter until soft. Add the Marsala and cook, stirring, until the alcohol has evaporated. Add salt and pepper to taste. Slowly add the cream, stirring as added. Continue to stir until heated. Set sauce aside but keep warm while you cook the spaghetti (*see p. 126*). When raw taste is gone but spaghetti is still slightly firm, drain it in a colander, add the mushroom sauce to the still-hot cooking pot, and return the spaghetti to it. Heat; add the parsley, put the pot over low heat, and quickly toss spaghetti in sauce. Serve at once, passing grated Parmesan cheese for each serving.

• *Makes 4 servings.*

NOTE: For double-quick preparation, put a big pot of water over high heat for cooking the spaghetti before you begin the sauce. Put the butter in a large (10-inch) skillet over medium heat before you chop the onion and slice the mushrooms. And, of course, use a food processor (if you have one) to chop, slice, and mince the vegetables.

★

Perfect Fettucini Alfredo

The secret of superb fettucini Alfredo is very simple: superb ingredients treated with the respect they deserve. Serve with a salad of Bibb lettuce, and remember, good pasta deserves a good wine.

¼ lb. imported Parmesan cheese, in one piece
1 small bunch very fresh, crisp parsley
1 lb. fettucini
4 Tbs. sweet butter, at room temperature
¼ cup heavy cream
Salt
Freshly ground black pepper

Grate cheese (no more than an hour before using); keep at room temperature. Wash parsley thoroughly, blot thoroughly dry. Remove tough stems (save for another use), chop leaves until very finely minced. Cook fettucini in a large pot of rapidly boiling water *(see p. 126)* until tender. Drain, return to hot cooking pot or to a very large (heated) bowl. Add butter, cream, cheese, and parsley; lift and toss fettucini until evenly coated with sauce. Season with salt and pepper. Serve at once.

• *Makes 4 to 6 servings.*

Fettucini with Shrimp and Broccoli

A really total meal; a dry white wine and crusty bread would be the perfect accompaniments.

1 bunch broccoli
Salt
4 Tbs. butter
3 cloves garlic, peeled, minced
½ lb. mushroom, trimmed, sliced
3 more Tbs. butter
1 lb. shrimp, shelled, deveined
1 Tbs. lemon juice
Salt
Coarsely ground black pepper
1 (1-lb.) package fettucini
½ cup freshly grated Parmesan cheese

Cut off broccoli stalks, reserve for another use.

Cut heads into flowerets, place in large bowl of salted water. Let stand 15 minutes, rinse well. Bring a large pot of water to a full boil, drop in broccoli and 1 tsp. salt. Bring water to boiling again, boil broccoli 1 minute. Drain in a colander, rinse with cold water. Set aside. Melt the 4 Tbs. of butter in a saucepan, sauté garlic and mushrooms until soft. Add butter, broccoli, shrimp, lemon juice, salt, and pepper. Cover and cook only until shrimp turn pink, about 5 minutes.

Bring a large pot of water to a full boil, add fettucini. Cook at boiling until just tender *(see p. 126)*. Drain and place on serving plates. Cover with shrimp-broccoli sauce. Sprinkle with cheese and serve at once.

• *Makes 4 servings.*

Pasta with Shrimp, Spanish Style

A lovely light Soave would be a great wine for this; add some crusty Italian bread and a fruit dessert.

2 Tbs. butter
2 Tbs. oil
2 medium-size mild purple onions, peeled, chopped
2 cloves garlic, peeled, minced
4 large ripe tomatoes, seeded, chopped
1½ lbs. raw shrimp, peeled, deveined, and coarsely chopped
½ cup chopped pimiento-stuffed olives
1 Tbs. chili powder
¼ tsp. marjoram
½ tsp. sugar
Pinch of cayenne
Salt
Coarsely ground black pepper
1 (1-lb.) package thin spaghetti

In a large skillet heat the butter with the oil until melted. Add garlic and onion, sauté until soft; add tomatoes. Cook, stirring often, 8 to 10 minutes. Add the shrimp, olives, and seasoning. Cook 2 to 3 minutes or until shrimp are pink. Keep sauce warm while preparing pasta. Cook spaghetti in a large pot of rapidly boiling water *(see p. 126)*. Drain, return to still-warm cooking pot, add sauce; toss well and serve.

   • *Makes 6 to 8 servings.*

Pasta with Zucchini and Ham

All that's needed here is a bottle of good Chianti. Have espresso and Italian chocolates for dessert.

3 Tbs. butter
3 Tbs. oil
2 cloves garlic, peeled, crushed

1 dry hot red pepper, seeded, pod split in half
4 small zucchini, trimmed, very thinly sliced
¼ lb. lean boiled ham, cut into narrow strips
½ cup minced parsley
Salt
Coarsely ground black pepper
1 (1-lb.) package fettucini

Melt the butter with the oil in a large skillet. Add the garlic and red-pepper halves; cook, stirring often, over low heat until garlic is deep brown and pepper halves dark. Remove and discard garlic and pepper. Increase heat to medium high, add zucchini and ham; cook, stirring, until zucchini is tender, 5 to 6 minutes. Stir in parsley, season to taste with salt and pepper. Keep warm while preparing pasta. Cook fettucini in a large pot of rapidly boiling water (*see p. 126*) until tender. Drain, ladle onto serving plates. Top with zucchini-and-ham sauce. Sprinkle grated Parmesan cheese generously over each serving.

• *Makes 6 servings.*

Green Noodles with Tomato Cream Sauce

With a main dish like this, who misses meat? A glass of Chianti would be a perfect accompaniment. Dessert could be espresso and Amaretti cookies.

6 to 8 medium tomatoes
4 Tbs. butter
½ cup chopped scallions or green onion
¼ cup chopped fresh basil leaves or 1 tsp. dried basil
½ pt. heavy cream, at room temperature
Salt
Freshly ground black pepper
Freshly grated nutmeg
1 (1-lb.) package green fettucini
Water
Salt
Oil

Plunge tomatoes into a large pot of rapidly boiling water, rinse under cold water, slip off skins. Cut each tomato in half, gently squeeze out seeds; cut halves into strips.

Melt butter in a large skillet, add scallions and sauté until soft; add tomatoes and cook, stirring, 2 to 3 minutes. Sprinkle with basil. Add cream; cook, stirring, until heated. Season to taste with salt, pepper, and nutmeg. Keep warm.

Cook fettucini in a large pot of rapidly boiling water *(see p. 126)*. When tender, drain and transfer to serving plate or shallow soup bowls.

Reheat sauce, ladle over fettucini, and serve at once.

• *Makes 4 servings.*

★

Pasta with Fresh Tomatoes, Ham, and Mozzarella Cheese

Serve with plenty of Chianti, some Italian bread, and possibly fresh fruit for dessert. Espresso for a finishing touch.

2 Tbs. butter
2 Tbs. oil
1 clove garlic, peeled, crushed
1 dry hot red pepper, seeded, pod split in half
4 large ripe tomatoes, peeled and chopped
½ tsp. dried basil
Salt
Pepper
1 lb. thin flat noodles
½ lb. mozzarella cheese, shredded
¾ to 1 cup shredded lean baked or boiled ham

Put butter, oil, garlic, and pepper halves in a large (10-inch) heavy skillet. Over low heat, stir with a wooden spoon until butter has melted. Continue stirring until garlic is golden brown, pepper halves dark; remove and discard garlic and pepper. Add sliced tomatoes and basil to skillet; bring heat to medium high. Cook, stirring occasionally, until tomatoes are very soft, about

15 minutes. Season with salt and pepper. Set aside and keep warm. Cook pasta *(see p. 126)* in a large pot of boiling water. Drain when tender but still slightly firm. Add the tomato sauce to the still-hot cooking pot and return the noodles to it. Place over low heat, add the shredded cheese and ham; toss quickly and serve at once.

• *Makes 4 servings.*

Fresh Tomato Sauce

Make this in midsummer, when fresh tomatoes are plentiful and inexpensive. Use part; freeze part to have on hand when garden-fresh flavor is what's wanted and needed.

8 to 12 medium to large ripe tomatoes
1 clove garlic, peeled, finely minced
1 medium-size mild purple onion, peeled, finely chopped
1 tsp. mixed Italian herbs*
1 tsp. salt
¼ tsp. coarsely ground black pepper
1 Tbs. sugar
1 to 2 dashes Tabasco sauce

Place all ingredients in electric slow cooker. Cook on low setting 1 hour. Stir; cook on high setting 4 to 6 hours, or on low setting 6 to 12 hours. Stir occasionally. To prepare sauce over conventional heat, place all ingredients in a large heavy saucepan, add 1 cup water. Cover and cook over low heat for 1½ to 2 hours, stirring frequently.

• *Makes 6 to 8 cups.*

NOTE: Sauce may be kept in refrigerator several days; reheat before using. Or it may be poured into 1- or 2-cup containers, sealed, and stored in freezer. Use within 3 months. Bring to a full boil before serving.

*Mixed Italian herbs are sold under various labels; often referred to as Italian seasoning.

The Bakery:
Breads and Cakes

WHILE DOZENS OF DIFFERENT FOODS are oven-baked—soufflés, casseroles, puddings, even vegetables—we concern ourselves here with bakery specialties; breads and cakes. Yes, I know, pies are traditionally part of the baker's art but, try as I will, I cannot in good faith include pies. The truth is, pie in the usual sense hardly fits into our new concept of lighter, more interesting food. And since I hope this book will truly offer you something new and fresh, there seems little point in giving recipes for ordinary pies which are probably duplicated in every cookbook on your shelf. You will find a recipe for cream puffs in the dessert section, but this is low in fat content and so delicious I couldn't leave it out. But pies in the usual sense simply do not seem to fit into today's menus.

Instead, here are easy homemade breads to be made in the usual way, by hand, as well as with that gift to the bread maker, the electric mixer with a dough hook. Here also is a new breed of cakes, requiring less time for the mixing than it takes to tell about it.

While it is certainly true that in some larger cities top-quality commercial breads and cakes are readily available, they are also inevitably expensive and never taste quite as incomparably good as home-baked. Like all the recipes in this book, these for baking are simple. They do demand first-class ingredients, but they do *not* demand either great skill or great amounts of time. The results, however, are very, very good.

BREAD

Perhaps nothing has changed so much these past few years as our taste in breads: there has truly been a revolution away from the dull, spongy commercial variety. A new awareness of good bread has tempted us all to the breadboard to produce our own crusty French, nutty-tasting whole-wheat, or firm, honest white loaves; to say nothing of hot rolls and fresh coffee cake to make an event of Sunday-morning breakfast.

Since there are now any number of new machines that will knead your bread without effort, even busy cooks are finding time to add interesting homemade bread to the new, simplified menus that are today's dining style. Quick breads, muffins, popovers, corn bread, and such are also definitely an old-new addition to the repertoire of today's cook.

The point now is to have bread add interest to the meal and complement the food being served; it should not simply be added to the table as a habit. The right bread can indeed make the meal, and it will well reward the cook to make the bread.

Basic White Bread

1½ cups milk, scalded
½ tsp. salt
3 Tbs. butter
3 Tbs. sugar
2 packages active dry yeast
½ cup lukewarm water (110°–115° F.)
5½ to 6 cups unbleached flour

In large bowl of electric mixer with dough hook combine hot milk, salt, butter, and all but 1 tsp. of sugar. Stir until butter has melted. Combine remaining tsp. sugar, yeast, and lukewarm water. Let stand until bubbly (5 to 10 minutes), add to mixture in bowl. Start mixer at low speed and add 5 cups flour, ½ cup at a time. Dough should be sticky at this point and start to cling to the dough hook. Continue to add flour, ¼ cup at a time, until dough is sufficiently stiff to leave the bowl and adhere completely to the dough hook. Let knead at low speed until smooth and glossy (8 to 10 minutes). Remove from mixer, form into a ball, and place in a large greased bowl. Turn to grease top of dough. Cover with plastic wrap and place in a warm, draft-free spot until double in bulk (about 1 hour). Punch down and shape dough into two 9 × 5 × 3-inch greased loaf pans. Cover and let rise until again doubled in bulk, 35 to 45 minutes. Place in preheated 350° F. oven and bake 30 minutes. Remove from pans to a rack and allow to cool before storing. May be frozen if desired.

  • *Makes 2 loaves.*

★

Crusty Italian Bread

  1 Tbs. butter, at room temperature
  1 Tbs. salt
  2 cups hot water
  2 packages active dry yeast
  ½ cup lukewarm (110°–115° F.) water
  6 to 8 cups unbleached flour
  ¼ cup cornmeal
  1 egg white beaten with 1 Tbs. cold water

In large bowl of electric mixer with dough hook attachment combine butter, salt, and hot water; stir until butter has melted. Dissolve yeast in lukewarm water, let stand until bubbly (5 to 10 minutes), add to mixture in bowl. Start blending mixture at low speed, adding flour ½ cup at a time until 6 cups have been added. Dough will be sticky, but at this point it will begin to leave the sides of the bowl and adhere to the dough hook. Continue to add flour, ¼ cup at a time, until dough leaves the sides of the bowl and adheres completely to the dough hook. Let knead at medium speed for about 5 minutes or until dough appears satiny and somewhat glossy. Remove from mixer, form into a ball, and place in a well-greased bowl; turn to grease top of dough. Cover and place in a warm, draft-free place. Allow to rise until double in bulk, about 1 hour. Punch dough down and shape into 2 long loaves. Arrange loaves on a lightly greased baking sheet that has been sprinkled with cornmeal. Place in a warm, draft-free place and again let rise until double in bulk. Place a shallow pan of hot water on the bottom of the oven. Preheat oven to 425° F. Bake loaves in preheated oven for 20–25 minutes; brush tops with egg white–water mixture. Turn off oven heat. Let loaves remain in oven until deep golden brown, about 5 minutes. Cool on racks.

★

Egg Twist Bread

This bread should actually be called "continental loaf," since it is very much like a type of bread one finds in many European countries. Slightly sweet, it is firm in texture but still a soft bread. It's very easy to make, and if preferred, can be shaped into plain French-style loaves or into big puffy rolls; but the braided loaves will make you look most professional.

> 1 cup milk
> ¼ cup (½ stick) butter, at room temperature
> 2 packages active dry yeast
> ½ cup lukewarm (110°–115° F.) water
> ⅓ cup sugar
> 1½ tsp. salt
> 3 eggs, slightly beaten
> 7 cups unbleached white flour
>   (plus additional flour if needed)

In a saucepan heat milk to scalding, pour into a large mixing bowl; stir in butter, cool to lukewarm. Dissolve yeast in warm water, let stand until bubbly; stir into milk mixture. Add sugar, salt, and eggs; stir to blend. Add 4 cups of the flour and beat to a smooth batter. Add remaining flour; knead until smooth. (If kneading by hand, add sufficient additional flour to prevent dough from sticking.) Form dough into a ball; place in a greased bowl, cover, and let rise in a warm place (80°–85° F.) for 1½ hours. Divide dough in half, let rest 10 minutes. Divide each dough piece into 3 parts, roll each part into a 12-inch rope. Braid, pinch ends to seal, and tuck under securely. Place diagonally on lightly greased baking sheet. Return the dough to a warm place;

let rise until nearly double—about 45 minutes. Bake in preheated 400° F. oven for 30 minutes.

• *Makes 2 loaves.*

Old-Fashioned Wheat Bread

Two superb, wheaty loaves of bread, the fashionable old-fashioned kind now served in elegant restaurants. The recipe is from a booklet published by the Wheatena Cereal Company.

2 packages active dry yeast or 2 Tbs. granular yeast
½ cup lukewarm (110°–115° F.) water
3 cups unbleached white flour
1 cup uncooked Wheatena cereal
2 Tbs. sugar
2 tsp. salt
2 Tbs. butter, at room temperature
3 to 3½ more cups flour

In large mixing bowl of electric mixer with dough hook, or in large bowl, dissolve yeast into water and let stand until bubbly —about 5 minutes. Add the 3 cups flour, the Wheatena, sugar, salt, and butter; beat until smooth. Beat in 3 cups more flour, knead until smooth. If kneading with a mixer, sprinkle gradually with most of the remaining flour during the kneading. If kneading by hand, turn dough out onto a floured board and sprinkle with remaining flour to prevent sticking.

Put dough in a greased bowl, cover, and let rise in a warm place (80°–85° F.) for 1 hour or until doubled. Punch down, cover, and let rise again for 30 minutes. Divide into 2 pieces and roll each into a ball. Let rise 10 minutes. Shape into loaves and place each in a well-greased 9¼ × 5¼ × 2¾-inch loaf pan. Return to warm place and let rise 50 to 55 minutes.

Bake in a preheated 425° F. oven 30 to 35 minutes. Turn out loaves onto a rack to cool.

• *Makes 2 loaves.*

French-Style Crusty Rolls

These are indispensable: they are the perfect rolls whenever the menu calls for crusty bread. Excellent with cheese for dessert.

½ cup milk
1 cup water
2 Tbs. butter, at room temperature
1 tsp. salt
2 packages active dry yeast
1 Tbs. sugar
½ cup lukewarm (110°–115° F.) water
2 cups unbleached white flour
1½ cups whole-wheat flour

Heat milk and water to scalding, add butter and salt, cool to lukewarm. Rinse bowl and dough hook of electric mixer with hot water; dry. Place yeast and sugar in bowl, add lukewarm water; let stand until yeast dissolves and small bubbles appear on surface. Add lukewarm milk mixture and the 2 cups white flour. Blend about 1 minute on low speed. Add remaining flour, blend until dough clings to hook and cleans side of bowl. Let knead 7 to 10 minutes or until dough is smooth and elastic; it will be slightly sticky to the touch. Form dough into a ball; place in a clean, well-greased bowl, turning to coat top with vegetable oil or soft butter. Cover, let rise in a warm, draft-free place until double in bulk, about 1 hour.

Punch dough down; let rest for about 5 minutes. Roll out on a lightly floured surface into a rectangle, approximately 9 × 14 inches. With a floured knife, cut into 2 × 3-inch rectangles. Place, not touching, on a greased baking sheet. Let rise in a warm, draft-free place until double in bulk, about 1 hour.

Bake in preheated 375° F. oven 15 minutes or until rolls are lightly browned. Remove from baking sheet and let cool on wire racks.

    • *Makes about 1 dozen rolls.*

Skillet Corn Bread with Bacon

A double-quick-to-make bread, great with salads, slow-cooked bean dishes, and stews. Serve it too instead of rice, under creamed chicken, jambalaya, and such.

    4 slices lean bacon
    1 cup yellow cornmeal
    1 cup unbleached flour
    1 tsp. baking powder
    ½ tsp. baking soda
    1 egg
    1½ cups buttermilk

Preheat oven to 400° F. In a 10-inch heavy iron skillet (or other heavy skillet with heatproof handle), cook bacon over low heat until crisp. Remove bacon; drain on paper toweling, crumble, and set aside. Pour 2 Tbs. rendered bacon fat from the skillet; set aside. Pour off and discard all but a thin film of the remaining fat from the skillet. Place skillet in preheated oven. Put cornmeal, flour, baking powder, and soda in a large bowl; stir to mix. · Make a well in the center. Pour buttermilk into well, add egg; blend into dry ingredients. Add reserved bacon fat and crumbled bacon. Pour into heated skillet. Bake in preheated oven 20 to 25 minutes or until firm and lightly browned.

 • *Makes 6 to 8 servings.*

Southern Popovers

    1 Tbs. vegetable shortening
    1 cup all-purpose flour
    1 cup milk
    2 eggs
    ½ tsp. sugar
    Dash salt

Preheat oven to 450° F. Grease two 6-cup muffin tins generously with vegetable shortening. Place in preheated oven for 3 minutes.

Combine remaining ingredients; beat with electric mixer just until smooth.

Remove muffin tins from oven, quickly fill half full with batter. Return tins to oven immediately. Bake 25 minutes (do not open oven door). Serve while still hot.

• *Makes 12 popovers.*

New South Biscuits

  1¼ cups all-purpose flour
  ¼ tsp. soda
  1 tsp. sugar
  1 (8-oz.) carton sour cream

Preheat oven to 450° F. Lightly grease a baking sheet.

Combine ingredients in a bowl, stir until smooth. Turn dough out onto a lightly floured surface, pat with floured fingers to ½-inch thickness. Cut with 2-inch biscuit cutter; place on greased baking sheet. Bake in preheated 450° F. oven 10 to 12 minutes or until golden brown.

• *Makes 8 biscuits.*

Mix-Ahead Honey Bran Muffins

These are delicious muffins you can "mix up" ahead and have ready to bake any time you're in the mood for a muffin.

  2 cups milk
  1 tsp. vinegar
  3 cups All-Bran cereal
  1 cup boiling water
  ½ cup vegetable oil
  ¾ cup honey
  2 eggs, beaten
  2½ cups unbleached white flour
  2½ tsp. baking soda
  1 tsp. salt

Combine milk and vinegar, let stand at room temperature until ready to use. Put bran in a large bowl, add boiling water; mix well, let stand 30 minutes. Add remaining ingredients, mix thoroughly.

This batter can now be stored in the refrigerator up to 3 weeks.

To bake: fill greased muffin cups ⅔ full. Bake in preheated oven at 400° F. for 15 to 20 minutes.

- *Makes about 3 dozen muffins.*

LE GÂTEAU

Sugary frosted cakes have somewhat disappeared from our menus lately; no one wants anything so sweet or has time to make it. Yet a homemade cake on hand in the freezer does solve impromptu dessert problems. It's also nice to have for that spur-of-the-moment cup of tea or coffee. My answer is what I call the "mix-it-all-at-once cake." All the ingredients are dumped into a big bowl, beaten well with an electric mixer, poured into a prepared pan, and baked. Once out of the oven and cooled, the cake is given a light glaze or a sprinkling of spirits. That's all there is to it: no creaming butter and sugar, then beating eggs; no sifting of flour and adding alternately with liquid. None of that. The whole thing can be made from start to oven in 10 minutes or less. And these are real cakes: real butter-and-egg homemade cakes, not tinny-tasting cake-mix cakes with their dry, crumbly texture; but velvet-smooth, luscious cakes to form the basis for any number of sophisticated desserts. They can be served with sweetened whipped cream well laced with liqueur, with sour cream and fruit, or simply solo with a cup of after-dinner coffee. Because they are real butter cakes, each one "keeps," either in the refrigerator or freezer, to be ready when you are for a sweet finale to any meal.

Peanut Butter Cake

Cake
3/4 cup (1 1/2 sticks) butter
1/4 cup chunky peanut butter
2 cups sugar
3 tsp. baking powder
3 cups all-purpose flour
4 eggs
1 tsp. vanilla
1/2 cup buttermilk
1/2 cup water

Peanut Butter Topping
1/4 cup peanut butter
1 cup confectioners' sugar
4 to 5 tsp. buttermilk

Bring all ingredients to room temperature (butter should be sufficiently soft to lift with a spoon). Preheat oven to 350° F. Generously grease and flour a 10-inch tube pan. In a large bowl combine all cake ingredients. Beat at medium speed for 2 to 3 minutes, occasionally scraping down sides of bowl and pushing batter toward beaters to blend thoroughly. Pour into prepared pan. Bake in preheated oven for 45 minutes. Reduce heat to 325° F. and bake a final 15 to 20 minutes or until food pick inserted in center of cake comes out clean. Cool in pan on rack about 10 minutes. Turn out onto rack, cool completely before frosting top of cake with Peanut Butter Topping.

To prepare Peanut Butter Topping
Combine ingredients, blend until smooth.

Cream Cheese Loaf Cake

¾ cup (1½ sticks) butter
1 (3-oz.) package cream cheese
1½ cups sugar
3 eggs
1¾ cups all-purpose flour
⅛ tsp. salt
½ tsp. almond extract
½ tsp. vanilla

Bring all ingredients to room temperature (butter should be sufficiently soft to lift with a spoon). Preheat oven to 325° F. Generously grease and flour a 9¼ × 5¼ × 2¾-inch loaf pan. In a large mixing bowl combine all ingredients. Beat at medium speed for 2 to 3 minutes, occasionally scraping down sides of bowl with a plastic spatula and pushing batter toward beaters to blend batter thoroughly. Pour into prepared pan. Bake in preheated oven 1 hour; reduce oven temperature to 300° F. and continue to bake 30 minutes or until food pick inserted in center of cake comes out clean. Cool in pan on rack 10 minutes before turning out onto rack. Cool completely. To serve, slice very thinly; serve plain with coffee, tea, sherry, or white wine. Or top cake slices with fresh fruit such as sliced strawberries or peaches and cover each slice with a scoop of vanilla ice cream.
 • *Makes 1 loaf cake.*

★

Mississippi Mud Cake

Cake

¾ cup (1½ sticks) butter
1½ cups sugar
2 tsp. baking powder
½ cup cocoa
½ tsp. salt
1¾ cups all-purpose flour

½ cup heavy cream
½ cup coffee
4 eggs
1 tsp. vanilla

Topping

3 cups miniature marshmallows
4 (1.2-oz.) chocolate candy bars, each broken
into small pieces

Bring all ingredients to room temperatures (butter should be sufficiently soft to lift with a spoon). Preheat oven to 350° F. Generously grease and flour a 12 × 9 × 2-inch baking pan. In large bowl combine all cake ingredients. Beat at medium speed 2 to 3 minutes, occasionally scraping down sides of bowl with a plastic spatula and pushing batter toward beaters to mix thoroughly. Pour into prepared pan. Bake in preheated oven 30 minutes or until a food pick inserted in cake comes out clean. Cover top of cake evenly with marshmallows and pieces of candy; continue to bake until marshmallows are lightly browned, candy partially melted. Cool, cut into squares, serve from the pan.
 • *Serves 8 to 12.*

★

Tropical Pineapple Cake

Cake

2 cups all-purpose flour
1 cup graham-cracker crumbs
1½ cups firmly packed brown sugar
1 tsp. baking powder
1 tsp. baking soda
1 cup (2 sticks) butter
1 (8¼-oz.) can crushed pineapple
2 Tbs. apricot preserves
½ cup orange juice (fresh is best)
3 eggs

Glaze
> ½ cup apricot jam
> ½ cup orange juice (fresh is best)

Topping
> 1 (3-oz.) package slivered almonds

Bring all ingredients to room temperature (butter should be sufficiently soft to lift with a spoon). Preheat oven to 350° F. Generously grease and flour a 10-inch tube pan. In a large bowl combine all cake ingredients; beat at medium speed for 2 to 3 minutes, occasionally scraping down sides of bowl with a plastic spatula and pushing batter toward beaters to mix thoroughly. Pour into prepared pan. Bake in preheated oven 1 hour to 1 hour and 10 minutes, or until food pick inserted in center comes out clean. Cool in pan on rack for about 10 minutes. Turn out onto serving plate. Spoon hot glaze over surface, sprinkle immediately with slivered almonds.

To prepare Glaze
    In a small saucepan combine preserves and orange juice. Stir over moderate heat until preserves are melted, mixture bubbly.

Southern Applesauce Cake

> ½ cup (1 stick) butter
> 1 cup firmly packed light brown sugar
> 2½ cups flour
> ¼ cup wheat germ
> 2 tsp. baking soda
> ¼ tsp. salt
> 2 cups (canned, sweetened) applesauce
> 2 large eggs
> 1 (3-oz.) can walnut pieces, finely chopped
> ¼ cup bourbon whiskey (or substitute apple cider or
>   unsweetened apple juice)

Bring all ingredients to room temperature (butter should be sufficiently soft to lift with a spoon). Heat oven to 325° F. Generously grease and flour a 9¼ × 5¼ × 2¾-inch loaf pan. In large bowl, combine all cake ingredients except nuts; beat 3 minutes at medium speed. Stir in nuts. Pour into prepared pan. Bake 1 hour or until food pick inserted in center comes out clean. Cool upright in pan on rack 10 minutes. Invert onto rack, cool completely.

• *Makes 1 loaf cake.*

NOTE: If you like, pour about ¼ cup bourbon or apple cider over cake when it is removed from the pan.

Poppy-Seed Cake

    1 (2-oz.) jar poppy seeds
    ¾ cup milk
    ¾ cup (1½ sticks) butter
    1¼ cups sugar
    3 eggs
    1 tsp. vanilla
    2 tsp. baking powder
    2 cups flour
    Confectioners' sugar

In a large mixing bowl combine poppy seeds and milk; let stand at room temperature 3 to 4 hours. Bring all remaining ingredients to room temperature. Preheat oven to 350° F. Generously grease and flour a 10-inch tube pan. Add room-temperature cake ingredients to milk–poppy seed mixture. Beat at medium speed about 1 minute, occasionally scraping down sides of bowl with a plastic spatula and pushing batter toward beaters to blend thoroughly. Pour into prepared pan, bake in preheated oven 30 minutes or until food pick inserted in center comes out clean. Cool in pan on rack about 5 minutes, invert and turn out onto cake rack. Cool. Dust with confectioners' sugar. Serve plain or topped with whipped cream.

• *Makes one 10-inch cake.*

Cherry Torte

Cake

>   2 cups all-purpose flour
>   1 tsp. baking powder
>   ¼ tsp. baking soda
>   1¾ cups quick-cooking oatmeal
>   1 cup firmly packed light brown sugar
>   ¾ cup (1½ sticks) butter, cold but not frozen

Filling

>   1 (1-lb. 5-oz.) can cherry-pie filling

Preheat oven to 350° F. Dump all cake ingredients into a bowl; with a pastry cutter or knife, cut butter into other ingredients until mixture resembles coarse crumbs. Place about ¾ of mixture in an ungreased 12 × 9 × 2-inch baking pan. With fingers, press out evenly; spoon pie filling on top and with a wet knife spread out evenly, leaving about ¼ inch around edges of pan uncovered. Cover pie filling as completely and evenly as possible with remaining mixture; press down lightly. Bake in preheated oven 35 to 40 minutes or until surface is very lightly browned. Cool in pan, cut into squares.

> • *Makes 8 to 12 servings.*

Sour Cream Cake with Coconut Topping

Cake

>   1 (8-oz.) carton sour cream
>   ¾ cup sugar
>   2 tsp. baking powder
>   1½ cups flour
>   2 eggs
>   1 tsp. almond extract (or substitute lemon extract)

Coconut Topping

> 2 Tbs. sour cream
> 2 Tbs. butter
> ½ cup brown sugar
> ½ cup grated coconut

Bring all ingredients to room temperature. Preheat oven to 350° F. Generously grease and flour an 8-inch square baking pan. Remove and reserve 2 Tbs. sour cream for topping. In a large bowl combine remaining sour cream and all other cake ingredients. Beat at medium speed 2 to 3 minutes, occasionally scraping down sides of bowl with a plastic spatula and pushing dough toward beaters to mix thoroughly. Pour into prepared pan. Bake in preheated oven 25 minutes. Cover top of cake evenly with coconut topping, bake a final 10 minutes. Cool in pan on rack. Cut into squares, serve from the pan.

To prepare Coconut Topping
   Combine all ingredients, blend well.

Walnut Cheesecake

> ¾ cup (1½ sticks) unsalted butter, cut into pieces
> ½ lb. cottage cheese
> 6 egg yolks
> ½ cup ground walnuts
> 2 Tbs. light rum
> 6 egg whites
> ¾ cup sugar

Preheat oven to 350° F. Butter and flour a deep 8-inch cake pan thoroughly; invert and shake out excess flour.

Place butter, cottage cheese, and egg yolks in food processor, process until smooth; pour into a bowl, stir in walnuts and rum. Beat egg whites and sugar until they hold firm peaks; fold into cheese mixture. Pour into prepared pan. Bake in preheated oven 1 hour or until a food pick inserted in center comes out clean. Cool in pan on rack; when cool invert onto rack. Refrigerate 6 to 8 hours or longer. Invert onto cake plate just before serving.
   • *Makes 6 to 8 very rich servings.*

Entremets—or
Just Desserts

To MY MIND the best desserts in the world are not prepared—
they are *assembled.* That sounds easy, doesn't it? But truth to
tell, really superlative assembled desserts require both knowl-
edge and skill, for the results depend on what's assembled, not
how it is done.

Let us take that queen of desserts, fruit with cheese. It can
be a disaster of hard, sharp-tasting cheese and unripe, unsuitable
fruit; or it can be a virtual poem with a creamy, almost melting
cheese and sinfully ripe fruit. Knowing your ingredients is the
key. Take the trouble to shop for a really ripe cheese and the
perfect fruit and, to accompany both, real French-style crusty
bread or rolls. With all, a velvet-tasting red wine. At the opposite
end of the scale there is that classic dessert of the finest of
chocolates accompanied by a silky cognac, with small cups of
strong, fragrant hot coffee—a chocolate bar with a cup of instant
is *not* a substitute.

However, any number of desserts, while they do require a
bit of preparation, are really almost assembled, taking little time
or trouble; they are simple and simply, beautifully, good. A great
meal deserves a great finale. Here are my favorites: perhaps they
will become yours.

Four-Minute Strawberry Cream

Zest (yellow skin) from 1 small lemon, cut into strips
2 (10-oz.) packages frozen strawberries
1 pt. sour cream

Put lemon strips in work bowl of food processor, process until grated. Break up or cut frozen strawberries into pieces about 2 inches in size, add to work bowl. With the machine running, pour the sour cream through the feed tube. Continue processing until mixture is just smooth. Transfer to a long shallow dish; place in freezer compartment of refrigerator until ripened and firm, about 45 minutes. Beat with fork just before serving.
• *Makes 6 to 8 servings.*

NOTES: If preferred, you may freeze this cream, following manufacturer's instructions, in your ice-cream freezer. It will taste best if transferred to the freezer compartment of your refrigerator when frozen and left to ripen and mellow about 1 hour before serving.

Variations

Four-Minute Raspberry Cream

2 (10-oz.) packages frozen raspberries
1 pt. heavy cream

Follow instructions for Four-Minute Strawberry Cream.

Four-Minute Raspberry Yogurt

2 (10-oz.) packages frozen raspberries
2 (8-oz.) cartons lemon yogurt

Follow instructions for Four-Minute Raspberry Cream above.

Russian Cream with Strawberries

2 envelopes unflavored gelatin
½ cup milk
1½ more cups milk
½ cup light brown sugar, packed down
½ pt. sour cream
1 tsp. vanilla
1 pt. fresh strawberries, washed, hulled
2 Tbs. sugar
2 Tbs. orange liqueur or brandy

Sprinkle gelatin over ½ cup milk, set aside. In a saucepan combine 1½ cups milk and brown sugar; stir over moderate heat until sugar has dissolved and mixture is hot. Stir in softened gelatin, stir until dissolved; cool. Stir in sour cream and vanilla. Pour into 6 individual ½-cup molds. Refrigerate until firm. Slice strawberries, add sugar and liqueur. Let stand at room temperature 1 to 2 hours. Unmold "creams," spoon sliced strawberries over and around.
   • *Makes 6 servings.*

Cottage Cheese Soufflé

4 Tbs. butter
1½ lbs. pot cheese or dry cottage cheese
¼ cup sugar
4 egg yolks
1 tsp. lemon juice
1 tsp. grated lemon peel
4 egg whites
¼ cup more sugar
Fresh Strawberry Lemon Sauce *(see opposite page)*

Fresh Strawberry Lemon Sauce

> 1 pt. fresh strawberries, washed and sliced
> ½ small lemon, seeded and chopped
> 1 cup sugar

Coat a 1½-qt. soufflé mold generously with butter. Preheat oven to 375° F. Melt butter, cool. Put cottage cheese in food processor, process until smooth; or put cheese through a sieve. Add cooled melted butter, ¼ cup sugar, egg yolks, lemon juice, and lemon rind; process or blend until thoroughly mixed. Beat egg whites until they begin to hold shape; add ¼ cup sugar a little at a time and beat until soft peaks form. Fold into cheese mixture. Pour into prepared mold; bake in preheated oven about 1 hour or until firm and well puffed. Serve with Fresh Strawberry Lemon Sauce.

To prepare Fresh Strawberry Lemon Sauce
Combine ingredients. Stir over low heat until sugar dissolves and mixture boils. Reduce heat, let simmer about 5 minutes. Serve warm or well chilled.

Cointreau Soufflé

> 2 cups pound-cake crumbs
> ¼ cup Cointreau liqueur
> 8 eggs
> 1 cup granulated sugar
> ⅓ cup more Cointreau liqueur
> 1 Tbs. grated orange rind

Butter and coat with sugar the inside of a 6-cup soufflé dish. Collar dish by wrapping lengthwise-folded brown paper around dish enough to overlap and to extend several inches above top of dish; secure tightly with string.

Soak pound-cake crumbs in ¼ cup of the liqueur. Separate eggs. Over hot water in double boiler, beat egg yolks with sugar until mixture thickens and coats back of spoon. Stir in ⅓ cup Cointreau liqueur and grated orange rind. Remove from heat, set aside to cool while beating egg whites. Beat egg whites until stiff but not dry, fold into egg-yolk mixture. Spoon into dish alternate layers of soufflé mixture and liqueur-soaked crumbs, with soufflé mixture on bottom and top. Place in 400° F. oven, immediately turning down to 375° F., and bake 35 minutes or until puffed and golden brown. Remove collar before serving.

   • *Makes 8 servings.*

★

Broiled Bananas with Vanilla Ice Cream and Rum

   4 ripe bananas, peeled, cut in half lengthwise
   ½ lemon
   Dark brown sugar
   2 Tbs. unsalted butter, cut into slivers
   4 scoops vanilla ice cream
   4 Tbs. dark rum

Arrange bananas on a foil-lined rack over a shallow roasting pan. Rub with cut side of lemon. Sprinkle generously with brown sugar, dot with butter slivers. Broil about 4 inches under high heat for 3 to 4 minutes, or until sugar is bubbly; watch carefully after about 2 minutes.

   To serve: Place a scoop of ice cream on each serving plate, arrange bubbly-hot banana halves (2 for each serving) on each side. With the back of a serving spoon make a well in ice cream; fill with rum and serve at once.

   • *Makes 4 servings.*

Apple Rum Crème

   1 (16-oz.) can applesauce
   ¼ cup light brown sugar
   ¼ cup light rum
   1 tsp. grated lemon rind
   2 cups graham-cracker crumbs
   1 pt. heavy cream

Combine applesauce, sugar, rum, lemon rind, and graham crackers; refrigerate until chilled. Whip cream until stiff; refrigerate until ready to use. Just before serving, fold applesauce mixture into whipped cream. Spoon into stemmed glasses.
• *Makes 8 servings.*

Meringue-Topped Apples

> 1 cup sugar
> Rind from ½ orange, cut into strips
> Rind from ½ lemon, cut into strips
> ½ cup Cointreau liqueur
> ½ cup water
> 6 tart apples, peeled, cored, cut into thick wedges
> 3 egg whites
> ½ cup more sugar
> Slivered almonds *(optional)*

Put the 1 cup sugar and orange and lemon rind in work bowl of food processor. Process until orange and lemon rind are finely ground; transfer to a large saucepan. Add liqueur and water; bring to boil, stirring. Reduce heat. Add apples, simmer gently until apples are soft but still hold their shape; spoon into individual casseroles. Beat egg whites until stiff, gradually beat in remaining sugar. Beat until light and glossy. Spoon over apple slices. Sprinkle with slivered almonds, if desired. Bake in preheated 350° F. oven 15 to 20 minutes, or until meringue is lightly browned. Serve warm or at room temperature.
• *Makes 6 servings.*

Apricots Imperial

> 1 (1-lb. 13-oz.) can apricot halves
> Rind from 1 orange, cut into slivers
> Juice from 1 large orange
> ¼ cup Grand Marnier, Cointreau, or other orange liqueur
> Vanilla ice cream

Pour syrup from apricots into a saucepan. Add orange-rind slivers and orange juice. Bring to boil, lower heat; let simmer 15 to 20 minutes or until syrup is reduced and quite thick. Add liqueur; pour over apricot halves in a glass bowl. Cover and refrigerate several hours. Serve in shallow dessert bowls topped with vanilla ice cream.

  • *Makes 4 to 6 servings.*

★

Prune Whip, Italian Style

> 24 pitted jumbo-sized prunes
> Boiling water
> Amaretto di Saronno liqueur
> ½ pt. heavy cream
> 8 ladyfingers

In a large bowl, pour enough boiling water over prunes to cover them by about 1 inch. Let stand until cooled to room temperature. Drain and place in a 1-pt. glass jar; fill the jar with Amaretto. Cover and refrigerate 2 or 3 days. When ready to serve, drain and chop prunes (reserve liqueur for another use). Whip cream until stiff, fold in chopped prunes. Split lady-fingers and arrange in 4 sherbet glasses. Fill glasses with whipped cream–prune mixture.

  • *Makes 4 servings.*

★

Bourbon Apples

> 4 large crisp apples
> 6 Tbs. light brown sugar
> Juice of ½ lemon, about 1½ Tbs.
> ½ cup bourbon
> 4 scoops vanilla ice cream

Peel, core, and cut apples into bite-size chunks; place in a large (10-inch) skillet. Add brown sugar, lemon juice, and bourbon.

Cover and simmer until apples are tender, stirring occasionally
and basting with liquid. Serve warm over scoops of vanilla ice
cream.

• *Makes 4 servings.*

Strawberry Clafouti

*Clafouti is the odd-sounding name for a French concoction;
part omelet, part soufflé, totally delicious. It takes about 10
minutes to prepare, about 30 minutes to bake. Served hot
from the oven or warm with vanilla ice cream, it's a sensa-
tional dessert.*

> 3 Tbs. butter
> 1 pt. large fresh strawberries, washed, hulled, cut in
>   halves or quartered
> 4 eggs
> 1¼ cups milk
> 2 Tbs. orange liqueur
> 1¼ cups flour
> ¾ cup sugar
> 1 pt. vanilla ice cream

Preheat oven to 350° F. In a heavy 10-inch skillet with heatproof
handle, melt the butter over low heat; cool. Pour into work bowl
of food processor, leaving a thin film of butter in the skillet.
Spread some of the butter up and around the sides of the skillet,
dump in the strawberries, and spread them out evenly; set aside.
Add the eggs, milk, and liqueur to the work bowl of food processor, process until blended. Add the flour and sugar, process
again until blended. Put the buttered skillet with the strawberries
over medium heat. When the butter starts to bubble pour in the
batter. Cook the clafouti on top of the stove for about 2 minutes,
then place it in the preheated oven and bake until well puffed
and lightly browned, about 30 minutes. Serve hot or warm with
a scoop of vanilla ice cream over each serving.

To make without a food processor: Combine melted butter,

eggs, milk, and liqueur. Beat well with a wire whisk, add flour and sugar, and continue to beat until very smooth and well blended.

• *Makes 4 to 6 servings.*

Tarte aux Cerises Flambé

(Flaming cherry tart)

> 1 (8-oz.) can pitted black Bing cherries
> 1 Tbs. sugar
> 1 Tbs. kirsch
> 2 large eggs
> ½ cup flour
> 1 Tbs. more sugar
> Pinch salt
> ½ cup milk
> 2 Tbs. butter
> ¼ cup more kirsch
> 2 Tbs. more sugar

Drain cherries; sprinkle with 1 Tbs. sugar, 1 Tbs. kirsch. Let stand 30 minutes; stir occasionally.

Preheat oven to 400° F.

Beat eggs until blended, add flour, salt, and 1 Tbs. sugar; beat with whisk to a smooth batter. In a saucepan heat milk to boiling; slowly add to batter, beating as added.

Melt butter in a 10-inch heavy skillet over medium high heat; pour in batter, let cook about 2 minutes. While batter cooks, drain cherries; reserve liquid. Sprinkle cherries over surface of batter. Place skillet in preheated oven; let tart bake 30 minutes or until well puffed and browned on top. A few minutes before tart is ready, combine remaining kirsch and sugar in a saucepan; add reserved liquid from cherries. Place over medium heat, stir until sugar dissolves. When ready, remove tart from oven; quickly bring kirsch syrup to a boil, ignite, and pour flaming over tart. Bring flaming to the table to serve from the skillet.

• *Makes 4 to 6 servings.*

Creme Puffs

Call them choux *if you must, but by any name they're heavenly for dessert. Bake them, freeze if you like, to have ready to fill with ice cream, to be laced with sauce for a fabulous instant dessert. Or bake, cool, and fill with flavored whipped cream. Freeze (tightly covered) until dessert is needed. Thaw 30 to 45 minutes before serving and top if you like with a sauce of sweetened pureed berries, given a little character with a jigger of cognac. Cream puffs may be made by hand, but each egg must be beaten separately in to the flour mixture very, very thoroughly.*

⅔ cup water
⅓ cup milk
½ cup (1 stick) butter
1 Tbs. sugar
¼ tsp. salt
1 cup flour
4 eggs

Preheat oven to 400° F. Lightly grease 2 baking sheets.

Combine all ingredients except flour and eggs in a saucepan. Bring to a boil, cook until butter has completely melted. Remove from heat. Stir in flour and beat until mixture is smooth and leaves sides of pan. Return to heat; cook, stirring, about 2 minutes. Immediately transfer mixture to processor work bowl. Add eggs, process until smooth and very thick. Stop machine and scrape down bowl once or twice. Drop by tablespoonfuls onto prepared baking sheets. Bake in preheated oven 22 to 24 minutes. Remove to racks, slit off tops to allow steam to escape. Cool before filling and serving.

• *Makes about 2 dozen puffs.*

THE MOST ELEGANT DESSERTS

And the easiest to prepare.

Apricot Crème

> 1 (8-oz.) package dried apricots
> Boiling water
> ½ to 1 cup sugar
> 2 to 3 Tbs. apricot brandy or liqueur *(optional)*
> ½ pt. heavy cream

Cover dried apricots by about 1 inch with boiling water; let stand several hours (overnight if you wish). Simmer over low heat until tender, about 10 minutes. Drain. Puree in food processor, or put through food mill or sieve. Add sugar to taste. Stir in brandy if desired; chill. Beat cream until stiff; fold in apricot mixture. Refrigerate until time to serve.
> • *Makes 6 to 8 servings.*

Chocolate Rum Mousse

> 3 eggs
> 6 oz. semisweet chocolate bits
> ½ tsp. instant coffee
> Pinch salt
> 2 Tbs. light or dark rum
> ½ cup sugar
> ¼ cup water
> ½ pt. heavy cream

Put eggs, chocolate bits, instant coffee, and salt in work bowl of food processor. Process until smooth. Combine sugar and water in a saucepan, stir over medium heat until sugar dissolves and mixture boils. With processor machine running, pour the hot sugar mixture carefully through the feed tube and process until smooth, about 20 seconds. Add rum and process 20 seconds more. In large bowl beat cream until stiff, fold in chocolate mixture. Transfer to individual dessert cups or to a serving bowl. Refrigerate until ready to serve.

To prepare by hand: Combine sugar and water in a saucepan, stir over low heat until sugar dissolves. Add chocolate bits, stir until melted. Remove from heat, add instant coffee and rum. Cool to room temperature. In bowl, beat eggs until light and frothy; slowly add cooled chocolate mixture, beating as added. Whip cream until stiff, fold in chocolate mixture.

Chocolate Strawberries

>1 pt. large, firm but ripe strawberries
>6 oz. semisweet chocolate bits
>1 Tbs. butter
>2 Tbs. brandy or Grand Marnier liqueur

Wash (do not hull) strawberries, blot dry. In top of double boiler combine chocolate bits, butter, and brandy or liqueur. Stir over simmering water until chocolate is melted and mixture smooth. Holding strawberries by stem end, dip one by one into chocolate mixture. Place, not touching, on lightly buttered baking sheet. Refrigerate until chocolate hardens. Serve on small plates, 5 or 6 for each serving.

Pears and Stilton

>4 ripe pears
>Lemon juice
>½ lb. Stilton cheese, at room temperature
>1 (3-oz.) package cream cheese, at room temperature
>1 to 2 Tbs. brandy
>8 walnut halves

Peel, core, and halve pears; brush with lemon juice to keep from discoloring.

Combine Stilton and cream cheese in a small bowl, blend and mash to a soft paste; add brandy and blend well. Pile mixture into pear halves, place walnut half in center of each. Refrigerate until time to serve.

NO TIME FOR DESSERT?

Here is a handful of "quickies" that will wind up any luncheon or supper with a flourish.

Sprinkle sliced ripe peaches or strawberries with brown sugar, top with sour cream.

Melt ½ cup of any tart jelly or jam, add ½ cup rum or brandy. Pour over ice cream.

Layer peeled, cored, and sliced apples in a shallow baking dish. Sprinkle generously with brown sugar, then with brandy, then with macaroon or Amaretti cookie crumbs. Dot generously with butter. Bake at 350° F. for 30 minutes or until apples are tender. Serve warm, with sour cream, if desired.

Combine 1 whole lemon, 3 eggs, 2 cups sugar, and ¼ lb. (1 stick) butter in a processor or blender. Process or blend until well mixed. Pour into six individual custard cups. Set cups in pan of hot water. Bake at 300° F. for 20 minutes or until set. Serve warm at room temperature. Decorate with whipped cream if you like.

Cut sufficient slices French bread to fit the bottom of a well-buttered 8 × 8 × 2-inch square baking dish. Sprinkle with ½ cup chopped dates, candied fruit, or raisins. Combine 3 eggs with 1 cup milk, ½ cup sugar, and 3 Tbs. brandy. Pour over bread, dot with butter. Set pan in a second pan of hot water. Bake 30 to 40 minutes at 300° F., or until custard is set and lightly browned.

Peel and cut navel oranges into even slices, layer in a bowl. Sprinkle each layer with fresh or frozen grated coconut. Sprinkle generously with Grand Marnier liqueur. Let stand an hour or two before serving.

Soak pitted dates and prunes in rum for several hours, stuff with pecan or walnut halves, roll in powdered sugar. Serve as an accompaniment to after-dinner coffee.

Combine 1 cup applesauce with 1 pint vanilla ice cream and ¼ cup bourbon whiskey. Freeze until almost firm before serving.

ICE CREAMS AND SHERBETS—

Or "Sorbets," If You Insist.

I scream, you scream, we all scream for ice cream. And well we might, for if the ice cream is homemade, it's something worth screaming for.

Fifty years ago, in a more leisurely age, people had both the time and inclination to hand-crank the ice cream freezer on the back porch, and homemade ice cream was a favorite Sunday dessert. But that day has passed, and until recently, homemade ice cream with it. Not any longer: there are wondrous new machines that do the cranking for us, and in a revolt against the chemical-laden commercial product, home cooks are making ice cream again.

Unlike most home-produced foods, your honest-to-freezer real ice cream is going to cost more than store-bought, but it is well worth the price. Even the best commercial ice cream cannot compare in flavor and texture to the make-it-yourself variety. What's more, you can be as inventive as you like about flavors, and that's very much part of the fun.

As if taste alone were not enough, nothing beats the luxurious feeling of having homemade ice cream on hand in the freezer. Great for party desserts or spur-of-the-moment treats: add a modest supply of liqueurs to your liquor cabinet, and you're ready for a really festive ending to any meal. Just try crème de menthe over fresh lemon ice cream, or a little brandy over burnt sugar. Super delicious!

One note of caution: Not that it's likely to happen, but don't try to keep ice cream too long; it will develop ice crystals. Serve it within a week after making. This is never a problem at my house; homemade ice cream is never around more than an hour, much less anything like a week—unless it is intended for a party, and then it has to be hidden.

Avocado Ice Cream

1 large lemon
2 large ripe avocados, sufficient to make about
    1 cup mashed avocado
1 cup milk
½ pt. heavy cream
½ cup sugar

Grate yellow zest from whole lemon; squeeze juice. Cut avocados in half, remove seed; peel and cut into chunks, place in food processor. Add lemon juice and rind.

Heat milk with cream to scalding; remove from heat. Stir in sugar, pour into processor over avocado mixture. Process until very smooth; pour into ice cream freezer container. Refrigerate until chilled. Freeze, following manufacturer's directions. Place in freezer compartment of refrigerator for several hours to allow flavors to mellow and ice cream to harden, if necessary.

• *Makes about 1½ pints.*

Burnt-Sugar Ice Cream

1 cup sugar
½ cup boiling-hot water
1 Tbs. instant coffee powder
2 Tbs. rum
4 egg yolks
1 Tbs. cornstarch
½ cup more sugar
1 pt. heavy cream

Place sugar in a large heavy skillet; stir over medium heat until dissolved to a deep golden syrup. Add hot water (sugar will harden), stir until sugar again dissolves and mixture is blended. Remove from heat, add coffee powder and rum. Stir to dissolve coffee, set aside. In top of double boiler combine egg yolks with cornstarch and sugar. Place over simmering water and beat with electric hand mixer (or rotary beater) until thick and about triple in volume. Remove from heat, cool. Cover mixture directly with plastic wrap; refrigerate until chilled. Beat cream until stiff, fold in cooled egg mixture and then burnt-sugar mixture; pour into container of ice-cream freezer. Freeze, following manufacturer's directions. Place in freezer compartment of refrigerator for several hours to allow flavors to mellow and ice cream to harden if necessary.

• *Makes about 1 quart.*

Cointreau Ice Cream

    4 egg yolks
    1 cup sugar
    2 Tbs. Cointreau liqueur
    1 pt. heavy cream

In top of double boiler combine egg yolks and sugar; place over simmering water. Using portable electric hand beater, beat at high speed until mixture is thick and about triple in volume; remove from heat, fold in liqueur. Cool, cover directly with plastic wrap; refrigerate until chilled. Pour into container of electric ice-cream maker. Freeze, following manufacturer's directions. Place in freezer compartment of refrigerator for several hours to mellow and harden if necessary.

• *Makes about 1½ pints.*

NOTE: Rum or other liquor can, of course, be substituted for the Cointreau.

Fresh Lemon Ice Cream

    2 large lemons
    2 cups sugar
    1 cup milk
    Yellow food coloring *(optional)*
    2 cups heavy cream

Trim ends of lemon, cut in quarters; chop fine in food processor or blender, or with sharp cleaver on wooden chopping board. Combine with sugar. Cover and refrigerate overnight. Add milk and 1 cup of the cream. Stir well (mixture will thicken). Add a few drops of food coloring if desired. Whip remaining cream, blend into mixture. Freeze in electric ice-cream maker according to manufacturer's directions, or freeze in foil-covered bowl in freezer compartment of refrigerator. When partially frozen, remove from freezer and beat well; return to freezer and freeze until solid.

• *Makes 1½ quarts.*

Philadelphia Cheese Ice Cream

    2 (3-oz.) packags cream cheese
    ½ cup milk
    2 egg yolks
    ½ cup sugar
    1 (8-oz.) carton honey yogurt
    1 (8-oz.) carton pineapple-orange yogurt

Break cream cheese into small chunks. Place with milk in food processor or electric blender. Process or blend until smooth.

In top of double boiler over simmering water, beat egg yolks and sugar with electric hand beater (or rotary beater) until very light and about triple original volume. Pour into processor (or blender); process (or blend) until combined with cream-cheese mixture. Add yogurts; process (or blend) until smooth. Pour into container of electric ice-cream freezer; refrigerate until chilled. Freeze, following manufacturer's directions. Place in freezer compartment of refrigerator (or in freezer) for several hours to allow flavors to mellow and ice cream to harden if necessary.

• *Makes about 1 quart.*

NOTE: To make by hand, blend cream cheese with a small amount of the milk until smooth. Add remaining ingredients and beat with a wire whisk until thoroughly blended.

Banana Rum Sorbet

    4 large ripe bananas
    1 cup milk
    1 cup sugar
    2 Tbs. dark rum

Peel and slice bananas; puree in a food processor (or in electric blender with about ¼ cup of the milk). Add sugar and process or blend to a creamy consistency; add milk and rum, blend. Put in ice-cream freezer; freeze, following manufacturer's directions.
    • *Makes 6 to 8 servings.*

Pineapple-Raspberry Sorbet

    1 cup water
    ¾ cup sugar
    1 (10-oz.) package frozen raspberries
    1 (1-lb.) can crushed pineapple
    2 Tbs. light rum

In a saucepan combine water and sugar; stir over medium heat until sugar dissolves. Boil for 5 minutes, cool. Thaw raspberries; puree in food processor or blender (or put through sieve or food mill). Combine puree with crushed pineapple, add cooled sugar syrup and rum. Freeze in ice-cream freezer, following manufacturer's directions.
    • *Makes 8 to 10 servings.*

Strawberry Sorbet

3 pts. strawberries
1½ cups sugar
1½ cups orange juice
½ cup lemon juice
2 Tbs. Grand Marnier liqueur

Wash, hull, and slice strawberries; combine in a bowl with the sugar and orange and lemon juices. Let stand at room temperature 2 to 3 hours. Puree mixture in electric blender or food processor (or put through a sieve or food mill). Stir in the Grand Marnier liqueur. Freeze in ice-cream freezer, following manufacturer's directions.

   • *Makes about 8 servings.*

Index